THE WAY TO SKI!

THE WAY TO SKI!

The Official Method

Stu Campbell, Max Lundberg & Professional Ski Instructors of America
Photography by Tom Lippert

THE BODY PRESS

Published by The Body Press
A Division of HPBooks, Inc.
P.O. Box 5367, Tucson, AZ 85703
(602) 888-2150
©1986 HPBooks, Inc.   Printed in U.S.A.
1st Printing

Book Design: Craig Brown
Illustrator: Ralph Harris
Editor: Carol Worth

Library of Congress Cataloging in Publication Data

Campbell, Stu.
The way to ski!

Bibliography: p.
Includes index.
1. Skis and skiing. I. Lundberg, Max. II. Lippert,
Tom. III. Professional Ski Instructors of America. IV.
Title.
GV854.C154   1986   796.93   86-62074
ISBN 0-89586-485-1 (hardcover)
ISBN 0-89586-444-4 (pbk.)

Contents

Acknowledgments

The photographs for this book were taken in July 1985 in the Glacier Bowl at the Mt. Alyeska Ski Resort, Girdwood, Alaska. This project would never have gotten off the ground without generous assistance from the management of Mt. Alyeska and dozens of other Alaskan hosts and supporters.

Particular thanks to Alyeska Mountain Manager, Dick Harris, who cheerfully trucked us, lugged mountains of gear, brought water, fuel and food, and even delivered a Polaris snowmobile to us by chairlift.

The skiers you see on these pages, are Carol Levine of Sun Valley, Idaho, and Jerry Warren of Snowbird, Utah. Both are members of the elite United States Alpine Demonstration Team sponsored by the Professional Ski Instructors of America (PSIA).

Without hint of complaint, Jerry and Carol prepared their own slopes, spread salt to firm the summer snow, hiked for every run, waited patiently for the sun to break through, then repeated maneuvers again, and again, and again for our camera.

The "eye" behind the lens was that of Tom Lippert of Truckee, California, *SKI Magazine's* photographer deluxe. Having worked with Lipp for so many years, we tend to take his extraordinary photography—and his ability to keep an entire crew "up"—for granted. His spirit is reflected on these pages.

The major part of this work is derived from lots of thinking and back-breaking work done by Paul Valar of Mittersill, New Hampshire, and by Horst Abraham of Vail, Colorado. Although the two represent different generations in the development of PSIA, together they must be considered co-founders of the American Teaching Method, which we now call ATM.

If these two represent ATM's origins, great teachers like Herbert Schneider, Sepp Ruschp, Alf Engen, Cal Cantrell, Roland Palmedo and many others must at least be considered major contributors.

Together with them, we must acknowledge the likes of Bill Lash, Doug Pfeiffer and Kerr Sparks, who had vision enough to found a national organization of ski instructors, and the courage to support it through its infancy.

Finally we thank all members of the PSIA Education Committee, past and present, and all coaches, racers and ski teachers from whom, wittingly or not, we have "borrowed" ideas.

Foreword

This book is about learning to ski—in the most straight-forward, efficient way possible. It's a no-nonsense, nuts-and-bolts ski lesson. As it begins, *The Way To Ski!* assumes you know nothing about the sport. It takes non-skiers by the hand, and leads them, step by step, along a learning path toward expertise.

It's a picture book. You will see hundreds of photos, arranged in sequences to let you trace, understand, and feel what's happening at each level.

We have kept the text as "short and sweet" as possible, eliminating, wherever we could, all high-tech jargon and complex theory. Most of what you read relates directly to the photos.

The photos are accompanied by short remarks, which appear in capital letters. These are the friendly directions a ski instructor might offer as you perform the lessons.

Please don't be misled by our book's apparent simplicity. The progression of skiing concepts we offer is based on millions of instructor-hours of practical experience.

It's also derived from exhaustive research, by some of the world's leading scholars in the fields of physics, biomechanics (the study of how the muscles, bones, and joints of the human body work), kinesiology (how our bodies perform when they're in motion), educational psychology (how people learn best), and ski mechanics.

Basically we, the co-authors, are both just ski instructors. We have been involved in ski teaching for longer than we'd like to admit.

Stu Campbell, formerly Educational Co-Chairman of Professional Ski Instructors of America (PSIA), is Director of Skier Services at Heavenly Valley, California/Nevada. He is also the technique editor of *SKI Magazine,* published in New York.

Max Lundberg, Education and International Vice President for PSIA, is an ex-member and coach of the U.S. Alpine Demonstration Team, and a frequent contributor to both *SKI* and *SKIING* magazines. For many years Max has headed the Alf Engen Ski School in Alta, Utah, and is listed among the finest powder-snow skiers in the world.

Stu Campbell (l) and Max Lundberg (r).

For all the other things we do, at heart we are merely students of the sport—learners like everyone else.

The Way To Ski! is designed to bridge the gap between apprentice ski instructors and the students they teach. Although it is not meant as the last word in advanced ski technique, it outlines a teaching progression approved by the PSIA.

It is offered to the general public—not as a substitute for ski instruction—but to let each reader understand where the skier fits into the scheme of things, and where to go from there. It's for that reason we speak to the student himself, rather than to the teacher.

Within the PSIA system, a student should be able to start lessons in Stowe, Vermont for example,

resume a month later in Vail, Colorado, and pick up the following season in Squaw Valley, California. Instructional standards should be the same everywhere, even though the system will vary slightly from school to school.

All lessons should have total continuity. We believe that the more the students know about their instructor and what they are to learn beforehand, the more valuable their lessons will be.

We also believe that ski teachers teach best when *they* are learning, and are excited about learning themselves. They teach worst when they decide they already understand it all and needn't grow further or ski better. *The Way To Ski!* should trigger growth in students and teachers alike.

Introduction: The American Teaching Method

The American Teaching Method describes the open-end system of instruction sponsored by the Professional Ski Instructors of America. PSIA, as we are called, is an amalgamation of ski instructors from around the world as well as the United States.

Although the term ATM implies a national ski technique, ours is not a strictly-defined system like that of Switzerland or Austria. ATM preaches that we must accept a good idea from any source—the only catch being that the idea must *work.* In that sense, the teaching philosophy adopted by most U.S. ski teachers is one that demands extreme flexibility and creativity on the part of the instructor. We believe in saying: "See where the student needs help, then give it. If that means deviating from the traditional teaching sequence, do it!"

The emphasis in *The Way To Ski!* is on the "how" and "why" of skiing. Learning by discovery is perhaps the essence of ATM. The more you discover, the more your skiing improves and the more you will recognize how much you have yet to learn.

We hope that as you read you will visualize, even feel, what you see on these pages. It will be most difficult, though, to catch the full dimension of the skiing experience through your reading. Only the feel of the snow, the cold wind in your face, and the sound of your own skis can give you that.

DEVELOPING SKILLS

When all other descriptions fail, skiing can be reduced to three things: gravity, friction and the movements of the skier.

Gravity

It's what lets us accelerate on a slippery incline—a snow-covered slope.

Friction

That's what lets us change direction and slow down.

Skier's Movements

Creating friction involves just three simple skills on the skier's part: turning, edging, and pressure control.

That's easy enough for anyone to understand. But the possibilities for how these basic skills are used in combination is infinite and complex beyond any single skier's ability to understand. We are all just learning to ski.

Turning is what is sometimes referred to as the "rotary skill." It happens when we apply rotary forces to our skis. There are plenty of these rotational forces at our disposal. Some are within our bodies. Some are external.

Some work better than others, and it's important from the beginning for each and every skier to understand, which allow us to ski correctly, and which can lead us into trouble.

Edging occurs whenever we adjust the way our skis relate to the snow. We can hold our ski flat so the plastic base faces the snow. If all or most of the ski's running surface glides on the snow, we have little or no "edge."

When we tilt the ski toward either of its steel corners, the edge digs into the snow and creates drag, or friction. The more we tip the ski off its base, onto its corners, the more we have "edged."

Pressure control can be done in one of two ways. First, we can use our muscles to apply more or less pressure to the skis. Second, we let the forces of turning and edging press against, or release pressure from, our skis.

Remember that a ski is a long slicing tool, like a flexible carving knife. It responds precisely to increases and decreases in pressure.

MILESTONES AND EXERCISES

Learning to ski is a never-ending process. You never reach your destination, because the "perfect turn" is always, like the end of a rainbow, somewhere near the horizon. But there are certain identity points along the way to ultimate technique. These we have called "milestones."

The milestones are not necessarily ends in themselves, but markers you should aspire to.

Not everyone follows exactly the same path up (or down) a mountain while working toward expertise—there are lots of ways to reach the summit. And not every ski teacher is likely to lead you along precisely the same learning route. The best teachers know all sorts of ways to get you there.

Exercises are useful learning aids—shortcuts and tricks to get you to perform (and remember) a movement pattern quickly. Every good ski instructor has a bag of tricks, and that bag usually grows bigger every day.

We have made no effort to mention every exercise that's ever been used to help a student reach a milestone. In fact, we probably don't even know half of them.

Think of the progression offered here as a skeleton, on which a limitless number of exercises, drills and practice runs can be hung to flesh out your skiing career.

If You Have Never Skied Before

Years ago a cartoon appeared in *SKI Magazine.* Two attractive ladies approach a ski instructor. One says, "I want you to teach my friend . . . I learned to ski yesterday."

Above the sketch, a caption might have read: *WHAT'S WRONG HERE?*

A couple of things. First, skiing is not something you "learn" in a day, a week, a season, or even in a lifetime. No one knows exactly how to ski. We're *all* constantly learning.

Second, there are thousands of great ski instructors. But a ski teacher is neither a magician, nor a miracle worker. Nobody can touch you with a wand and say, "Poof, you're a skier." Skiing correctly takes some time, good guidance and a certain amount of effort.

At first, you'll feel that skiing has a lot of things to cope with. There's the expense, the cold, and the unfamiliar equipment. Every single beginner has felt that way. It's perfectly normal.

The more you understand beforehand, the easier your first few days will be. And so the lady who speaks in the cartoon also does something *right*—she goes to a ski instructor.

The more typical scenario looks something like this: Friend "learns" how to ski. Anxious to share skiing with a buddy (wife, boyfriend, child), friend arranges ski trip. They arrive at ski resort, buy lift tickets, and ride chairlift to the top of mountain.

Friend proceeds to "teach" buddy to ski. Buddy is frightened and founders. Friend gets frustrated, then disgusted. They scream at each other. Eventually friend leaves buddy on mountain to fend for himself. Buddy gets injured. Dubious friendship damaged as well.

Alternate Scenario #1: Buddy survives, manages to make it down to base lodge in one piece. Cold, angry, and tired, he vows never to ski again. Another skier lost forever.

Alternate Scenario #2: Friend has patience enough to stay with buddy. Friend coaches buddy according to his perception of how skiing works. (The blind leading the blind.) Buddy develops hopelessly bad habits. Skis wrong for life.

These little dramas are played out, dozens of times, day in and day out at every ski resort in the world. If it weren't so sad, it would be a joke.

As a beginner, your judgment about who's a "good skier" and who's not is probably inaccurate. In fact, for your entire skiing life, anyone who's better than you are will seem to be a "good skier."

You will always be tempted to "take lessons" from skiers you perceive to be "good." Their intentions, and yours, may be only the very best. But resist the temptation. Nine times out of ten, learning to ski from friends is as counterproductive as teaching your spouse to play golf.

Take lessons from professionals.

SKI SCHOOLS

The ski instructor in the cartoon is depicted as a dashing figure. Ski instruction is seen by many as a glamorous job. It is, and it isn't.

Many good skiers who decide to become ski instructors are quickly disillusioned. Often their applications are simply not accepted. Good skiers don't necessarily make good teachers.

If they get hired, they find the training long, hard and sometimes ego-deflating. Their skiing is torn apart, and put back together piece by piece. They are taught to teach fundamentals from ground zero.

Those that survive the training, work long, sometimes difficult, hours. They are critiqued and evaluated constantly.

Those who are serious about the job, study to take their "certification" exam. It's not easy. A fully-certified ski instructor is qualified to teach anyone, at any level, on any terrain, in any kind of snow conditions. Many fail certification their first time out.

In short, good ski schools train instructors, as well as the general public. That's to your benefit.

LESSONS

Before you visit a ski area, drop the resort a note in advance, asking them to send you information about their ski school. With minor variations, you will learn something like this:

Most ski schools offer class lessons, private lessons and special children's lessons. As a beginner, you may want to look at class lessons first.

Class Lessons

A class lesson normally lasts two hours, though this may be slightly different at the area you visit. Usually there are morning sessions that begin at about 10 a.m., and afternoon sessions that begin at 2 p.m.

You may take both the morning and afternoon sessions—called a *full-day lesson*—or the *half-day lesson*. Some ski areas, where there is night skiing, offer lessons in the evening as well.

It's often possible to buy a series of prepaid class lessons—one a week, for instance, for several weeks. Don't forget that classes begin promptly at the appointed hour, so plan to be on time.

The number of people in a group lesson will vary. Sometimes there are as few as three or four. Sometimes, during busy vacation periods, there may be as many as a dozen or more. Usually, though, beginner classes have no more than eight to ten people.

In your first lesson you may not ride a lift at all, at least until the very end of the class. You will learn to walk and climb, as well as learn to control your speed and stop. While others climb, you ski, and vice-versa. You get to watch both the instructor's demonstrations and other students.

That's the advantage of a class lesson. You get plenty of chance to rest.

Private Lessons

Private lessons cost more because you get individual attention. You buy private-lesson time by the hour. When you're first starting out, a "private" may or may not be the best investment. You must decide based on how you feel about receiving instruction on an individual basis.

Privates are best for more advanced skiers, particularly those trying to break a bad habit or make it over a learning hump. You get to pick your instructor's brains while you're riding the lift.

Semi-Private Lesson

This involves two or more people with a private instructor. As a beginner, think carefully before arranging a semi-private. You must be compatible with your semi-private companions.

Children's Lessons

Children should not join an adult class. Special childrens' groups, instructors and learning areas are a major part of the curriculum at most ski schools. Normally the school asks that children be at least five years old before they can be accepted in the program.

Some ski schools offer all-day sessions for kids, which include skiing, snacks, games, lunch, and even an afternoon nap. This may be the best plan, particularly if you want to ski yourself.

Children younger than five often express interest in skiing. The best bet in that case is to arrange a private lesson for your three-year old or four-year old. But limit the lesson to just one hour. That's usually about as long as a very young child will last.

Prepare yourself. Your children will probably learn to ski much faster than you do. Don't hold them back. Let them learn as fast as they can. You may *never* catch up.

Don't be shy. Ask questions at the ski school desk. Ask the supervisors on the hill. Tailor lesson arrangements to suit your needs. There are usually plenty of options.

RENTING EQUIPMENT

There is no point in investing a lot of dollars in skiing gear before you start out. Rent equipment for a while.

Most ski areas have rental shops right on the premises. If not, there are surely local shops that have rentals available. You will need to rent skis, ski boots and ski poles. Some shops even rent jackets, hats and mittens.

The shop will probably ask you to fill out (and sign) a rental agreement. They will also ask for ID, and may require that you leave a credit card, a driver's license or a certain amount of cash as a security deposit on the equipment you will be using. Don't forget your wallet or purse.

You may wish to rent the gear for the day, the weekend or for several days.

Boots

First you will be fitted for boots. It's usually best to wear one pair of clean, smooth-textured socks. Take your time selecting boots. They should fit as well as possible. The boots are a critical connection between you and the skis. Ill-fitting boots can be torture chambers.

Here are things to look for:

♦ Ski boots that fit right may vary a size, or even as much as two sizes, from your street-shoe size.

♦ The boots will fit snugly, but should not bind or pinch anywhere. All buckles should have tension on them, but should open and close easily.

♦ Your big toe should be close to, but not touch, the front of the boot.

♦ The boot's "heel pocket" should hold your foot securely. If you can lift your heel off the boot's inner sole, the boot doesn't fit properly.

♦ At first ski boots will feel heavy and clunky. That's because they are—compared to regular foot gear. Walk around for a while to get used to them.

♦ Boots that fit well and feel comfortable in the

shop, don't always feel that way after several hours on the slopes. If your rental boots are giving you trouble, go back to the shop and exchange them for a pair that fit properly. That's better than blisters and sore feet.

Poles

Pole length is based on your height. The shop employee might stand a pole upside down on the floor next to you, and ask you to grip it underneath the "basket"—that circular part of the pole that keeps the point from sinking into the snow too far.

Holding the pole like this simulates the pole's length when it's sticking in the snow. When gripping the pole this way, there should be a 90-degree angle between your upper arm and your forearm. If that's the case, and your forearm is horizontal, the poles are the right length.

Experienced shop employees gets adept at sizing people up. They may simply hand you a pair of poles of the correct length.

Skis

The shop staff will also help you select the right length skis. Make sure you tell them you're a new skier. If you're a woman of average height your skis may be 125 to 135 centimeters long. A man of average height will start on skis that are 150 to 160 centimeters long.

In most cases this means the skis will reach a point somewhere between your chin and your nose when you stand them next to you.

Once you have skis, you must have your bindings adjusted. This will be done with your boots on—at a special adjustment bench. The binding is set to release the ski from your foot when (not if) you fall.

The adjustment setting is calibrated on the basis of your weight, your strength, and your skiing ability—in this case "beginner". Be honest with the adjuster when you are asked questions, and follow instructions. Watch closely so you understand how the bindings go on and off.

Once in a while, bindings are set too tight or too loose. If you or your instructor notice that your skis come off too easily (or they don't come off at all) be prepared to go back to the rental shop for a readjustment. It only takes a few minutes.

Don't try to adjust your bindings yourself, and do not expect your instructor to adjust them for you. Binding adjustment should be done by a trained specialist only.

Some newer rental equipment is designed so the boot and the binding are part of a single unit. In this case the adjustment will be preset. When you have a good boot fit, everything else is done automatically.

BUYING EQUIPMENT

After a few lessons you may want to buy your own equipment. It might be a good idea to take your ski instructor to the shop with you.

Spend the most time choosing boots. They are your most important single skiing investment. Use the guidelines offered above, and ask lots of questions. Try on many boots, flex them, and walk around in them for a long time.

You already know how to choose the proper-size ski poles.

Because your skills will grow into them, the skis you buy for yourself should be a little longer than those you rent for your first lessons. They should be equal to, or just a little shorter than, your height.

There may be a confusing array of ski models to chose from—within a broad price range. Get all the advice you can, not from friends who are "good" skiers, but from your instructor and well-informed shop clerks.

WHAT TO BRING

As a beginner, it's not necessary to show up for class in expensive, high-fashion clothing. That can come later. For now, jeans are fine, although an inexpensive and waterproof overpant would be better.

Instead of wearing a single heavy garment, it's best to put on several layers of clothing. "Layering" is an idea used by most experienced skiers. You can always be comfortable by taking things off or putting more layers on.

For instance, on top you might wear an undershirt, a regular cotton or wool shirt, a sweater or sweatshirt, and a thin windbreaker or insulated jacket.

On the bottom you may want longjohns, jeans, and some sort of overpants if you have them.

Here's a checklist and photo [1A] of what else to bring

1) Ski school ticket. (They won't let you in class if you forget it.)

2) Lunch money.

3) Mittens or gloves. Keep them on, even if you get hot. Scraped knuckles can be painful and slow to heal. Protect your hands.

4) Hat for warmth and/or sun protection.

1A

5) Sunglasses or goggles. The combination of high altitude and sunlight reflected off the snow can be overbright and damage your eyes. Protect them too.

6) Sunscreen. Even if you're a "tanner" on the beach, you can be seriously sunburned in the mountains. Wear sunscreen when you come out, and bring extra to put on later.

7) Chapstick.

8) Another layer, such as a sweater.

9) Small bag or rucksack for extra "stuff."

10) Poles and skis

11) Don't forget to go to the bathroom.

WHAT TO EXPECT

We can't help but judge and evaluate our teachers. A ski instructor is no exception.

The more you know about what to expect, the more you will get from your lesson. You should have high expectations.

Instructors should be leaders and guides, not drill sergeants. If they're good, they will put you in situations where it's easy for you to learn. Remember though, they can lead you to snow, but they can't *make* you ski.

Your teacher can guide your experience, in other words, but can't perform for you. The learning is up to you.

Grade your ski teacher on this report card:

♦ Appears neat? Clean? Well-groomed?

♦ Equipment. Clean? Well-maintained?

Up-to-date?

♦ Patient?

♦ Speaks well? Explains clearly? Can everyone always hear? Talks too much? Too little?

♦ Demonstrates well? Shows you *exactly* what was just described? More? Less? Something different?

♦ Stands in the right place where everyone can see? Where everyone can hear? Where everyone can *be* seen and critiqued?

♦ Critical enough? Points out what you do right, as well as what you do "wrong?"

♦ Does everybody in the class get equal treatment?

♦ Does your teacher recognize when people are getting tired?

♦ Keeps the class moving?

♦ Does the instructor let students learn at their own pace?

♦ Did you learn a lot? Do you feel that you can control your skis?

♦ Above all, did you have fun?

♦ Would you take another lesson from this teacher?

When the lesson is over, share your experience with the ski school. If you had a good time, say so. If you see room for improvement, offer some helpful feedback.

In time you may become friends with your favorite ski instructor. Keep in mind that your teacher is like your dentist. You should see your ski instructor at least once a year—even when you're an intermediate or expert skier—because bad skiing habits, like dental problems, can develop quickly.

The Basics

CLASS A

Are you just starting to read here, where the pictures begin?

If so, you're like most people who begin skiing for the first time—not fully prepared. Please go back to the previous chapter and spend a few minutes reading it.

GETTING READY

Here are some reminders:

- Don't forget to dress in layers.
- Don't forget a hat and gloves or mittens.
- Don't forget your sunglasses and sunscreen—even if it looks cloudy.
- Don't forget to go to the bathroom.
- Once dressed, put your ski boots on. The boot buckles go to the outside. Don't laugh. Plenty of people show up at the ski school meeting place with their boots on the wrong feet—embarrassing.
- Go through the checklist on pages 15 and 16.

2A.1

CARRYING SKIS AND POLES

Getting yourself and your gear from the rental shop or car to the ski school meeting place can be easy. Or it can be a big chore.

If you carry your skis and poles in your arms, clutched to your chest, everything will seem heavy, awkward and disorganized. At worst you will slip, stumble and drop everything. At best you'll be in a sweat by the time you get to class.

Make things easy. Carry your skis on either your right or left shoulder. First, stick your poles in the snow, or lean them against a wall so they're out of the way.

Place both skis on their *tails* (the back ends), with the *bases* (the running surfaces) together, and the *tips* (the front, pointed ends) up. [2A.1]

The skis will balance nicely on your shoulder if you carry them with the tips forward. To hoist them, grab both skis near the tips. Slip your other hand under the skis just in front of the binding [2A.2], and swing the tails onto your shoulder.

Slide the skis forward or back until they balance comfortably, then support them with your nearest hand. [2A.3]

2A.2

2A.3

Now pick up your poles. As you walk, you can carry the skis flat on your shoulder, as Jerry does here [2B], or with the skis on their sidewalls, like Carol. Grip both poles together, either near their tops, or somewhere near the middle. [2B again]

If you are walking through (or standing in) a crowd of people, carry your skis vertically in one hand. When you carry skis on your shoulder you risk hitting others in the head with your ski tails.

Putting on Equipment

At this point, even the slightest slope will seem like a precipice. When you get to the ski school meeting place, look for the flattest spot you can find, and swing the skis off your shoulder.

Your boots may pick up some snow during the walk to the ski school meeting area. If there is snow stuck to the bottom of your boots, your binding will not seem to "fit." Scrape or knock all the snow off your boot sole.

Most rental skis have no right or left binding. Either ski can go on either foot. Place your skis across the slope (if there is one), so they won't slide forward or back. Then get ready to step into the binding of the ski that's farthest downhill. [2C]

2B
CARRY SKIS WITH THE TIPS FORWARD

2C
ALWAYS PUT ON YOUR DOWNHILL SKI FIRST

Remember, once a ski is on your downhill foot, you can stand on it to put on the other. If you put your uphill ski on first, the downhill ski keeps sliding away from you as you try to step into it.

Try to recall the binding release check you went through in the rental shop. With some bindings you simply place the toe of your boot in the binding's toe piece, and step down with your heel. Make sure the binding is "open" first.

With other types of bindings you must kneel to "close" the heel mechanism. [See both types of bindings in 2C]

Most ski poles have leather or plastic straps. A few have sword-type grips with no straps. If you get rental poles made for the right or left hand, the difference will be obvious, so don't worry about which is which.

If your poles have a strap, lift up on the loop with one hand, and slip your other hand upward through the loop. [2D.1] Now reach down to grip the pole. The strap should be held between your palm and the pole grip, and the loop will be around your wrist. [2D.2]

If you have trouble with either your skis or your poles, ask for help. If you're on time for class, someone from the ski school will be there to assist you.

2D.1
REACH UP THROUGH THE POLE STRAP

2D.2
THEN GRIP DOWN

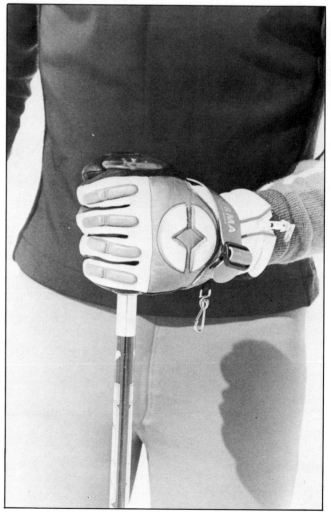

INTRODUCTIONS AND WARM-UP

At the beginning of ski school, students will stand in one place, and the instructors will stand in another, waiting to be assigned a class. To the instructors, this is known as *line-up.*

An instructor will come out of the line-up to greet you and others in your group and you will exchange first names. You will probably turn in your ski school ticket at this time.

The instructor will check everyone's boots and bindings, and make sure everyone's poles are on properly. You will then, as a group, move away from the ski school meeting area.

Because skiing is a winter sport, it's usually done in the cold. That makes warm-up especially important. Your instructor may lead you through a few simple exercises to loosen the muscles and get your blood flowing.

Priorities for you are very simple. The first concern is always for your *safety.* The second objective is that everybody have *fun.* Third is *learning.*

Throughout the lesson the instructor will be on the lookout for signs of *fatigue,* and will pace the lesson so nobody gets too tired.

Your teacher will also be very selective about the *terrain* you will ski on—choosing just the right portion of the slope will make things easier for you. That's why you will be asked to start and end your maneuvers in a very specific place.

2E.1
KEEP YOUR POLES BEHIND YOUR FEET

2E.2

2E.3

WALKING

Before you go anywhere all suited up and in full equipment, there are a few non-downhill basics you need to get comfortable with.

At first, start with one ski on if you like. Go forward, backward, and in circles.

To walk on two skis, you need to work your skis and your poles in combination. Your skis will feel long, heavy and, of course, slippery. If you try to walk up even the slightest grade you will slide backwards.

Your poles are extensions of your arms. They allow you to reach the ground without bending over or kneeling down. To keep from sliding backwards, always keep at least one pole behind your feet. [2E.1]

It's just like walking without skis. As you step with one foot, you swing the opposite arm forward. Give yourself a little push with your poles [2E.1 again], then slide your left ski forward. As your left ski moves ahead, your right hand and pole move forward. [2E.2]

Move along in a kind of shuffling motion, always keeping the *tip* of one pole (the bottom, where the point is) behind your feet. As the right foot shuffles ahead, the left hand reaches forward with its pole. [2E.3] Walk rhythmically, and say to yourself: "Opposite pole, opposite ski."

TURNING

With skis on, you suddenly have very long feet. Get familiar with the ski's tip and the ski's tail.

Stand still and steady yourself with your poles. Lift one foot, leaving the ski tip on the snow and raising the ski's tail off the snow. [2F.1] Don't lose your balance.

Now do just the reverse. Leave the tail of the ski on the snow, and lift the tip by pulling up with your toes. [2F.2]

2F.2
LIFT THE TIP

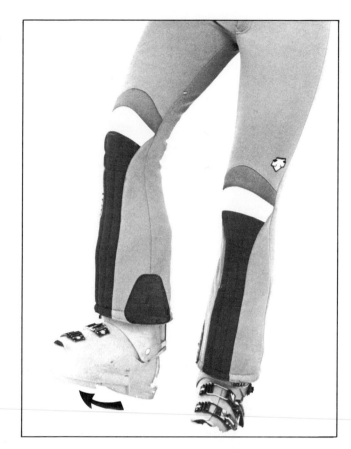

Repeat these moves several times—with each foot.
For practice, your instructor may ask you to take
your skis off, then step back into your bindings.
While your skis are off, you may be asked to turn the
toes of one foot to the outside—away from your
other foot. [2G.1]

Then turn your toes the inside—toward your other
foot. [2G.2]

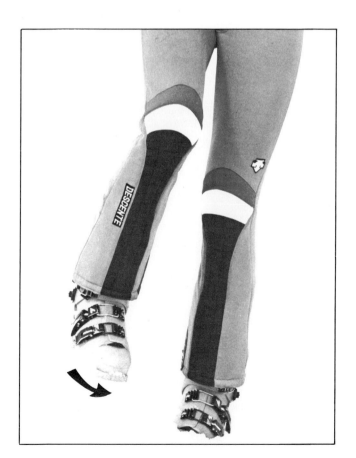

2G.2
TURN YOUR FOOT TO THE
INSIDE

Put your skis back on. Now lift one ski and point its tip away from the other. As you twist your foot the ski will pivot easily in the air. [2H.1]

Next, lift and turn your foot and ski the other way. This time the tip of the raised ski will cross over the ski that's still on the snow. [2H.2]

Remember what these turning movements feel like. They are basic to skiing.

2H.2
TURN YOUR SKI IN

21.1
ARMS APART

21.2
MOVE THE TAIL

21.3
BACK
TOGETHER

PIE TURN

To walk back to where you started, you need to reverse direction. To turn around, do what's called a *pie turn.*

The idea is to turn around without crossing your skis. Find a nice level spot. Spread your arms wide, and stick your poles in the snow. [21.1]

Leaving the tip on the ground, lift the tail of one ski off the snow and move it away from the other. Now your skis resemble a piece of pie. [21.2]

To bring your skis back together, stand on the ski you moved first, lift the other tail and move it close to the first ski. [21.3]

Remember to keep both tips of both skis on the snow. If part of each ski stays on the snow, the tips can never cross.

Make another pie-shaped step. First move one tail [21.4], and then the other. [21.5]

21.4
LEAVE YOUR TIPS
ON THE SNOW

21.5
STEP TOGETHER

Now you are up against your other ski pole. Spread your arms again, and move both poles. Make more pie-like steps (leaving your tips down), until you're headed back the other way.

Another way to do a pie turn is to spread your hands and plant your poles again. [2J.1]

This time, leave the *tail* of your ski on the snow, and move one tip away from the other. [2J.2]

Step the skis back together, always leaving both tails on the snow so the skis can't cross. [2J.3]

Step one tip again. [2J.4]

Then the other. [2J.5]

Move your poles and pie-step some more until you face the opposite way.

Practice walking. Practice both types of pie turns: (1) stepping around with your tips, and (2) stepping around with your tails.

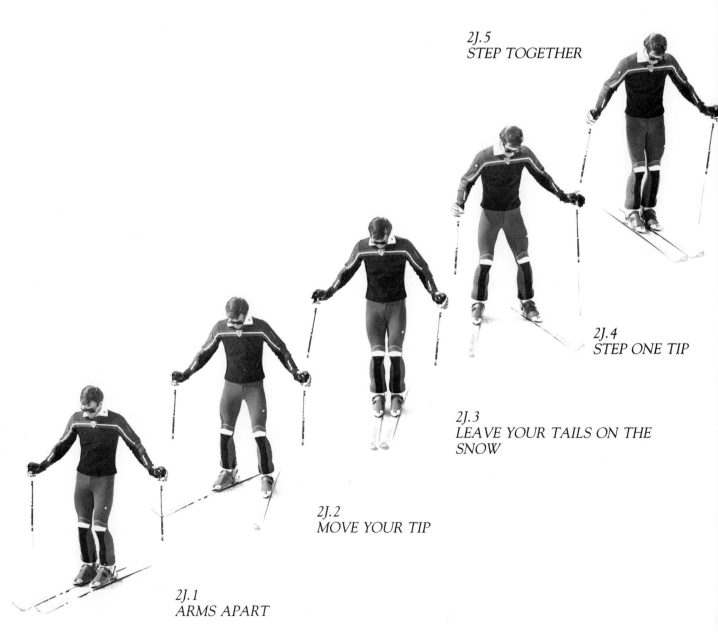

2J.5
STEP TOGETHER

2J.4
STEP ONE TIP

2J.3
LEAVE YOUR TAILS ON THE SNOW

2J.2
MOVE YOUR TIP

2J.1
ARMS APART

SIDESTEPPING

The *fall line* is a term you should understand. It has nothing to do with you falling.

The fall line is the fastest line down any hill. It's the route a ball would take, more or less, if you released it on a slope at any point. The fall line is rarely straight. Because slopes tilt, twist, and undulate, a ball alters its course, taking a curved path on its way downhill.

As a skier, you must always be aware of the fall line—where it is and how it changes. Some of your earliest skiing runs will be straight down the fall line. After that, though, you'll ski in the fall line only a small part of the time.

Gravity has its strongest grip on us when we're in the fall line. We go fast—sometimes too fast—in the fall line. So we learn ways to slow ourselves down, by skiing into, out of and back and forth across the fall line. This means we have to turn.

Even as you encounter a ski slope for the very first time, you must immediately visualize where the fall line is. Just walking up a hill, for instance, means you have to place your skis across, or perpendicular to, the fall line.

As you work your way uphill, keep your skis out of the fall line. If you let your tips point too close to the fall line, you start to slide forward. If you let your tails get too close to the fall line, you start to slide backwards. Such as when you try to sidestep.

Use The Fall Line

We hike uphill by *sidestepping*. The most important thing to remember while sidestepping is to keep your skis *across* the fall line. [2K.1]

How To Edge

Stepping sideways up the fall line may seem awkward at first. For one thing, you keep slipping sideways, back downhill. That's because you are holding your skis too flat on the snow. To keep from sideslipping you have to *edge* your skis.

Edging is easy. Simply push your knees uphill a little. By tilting your lower leg, you also tip the skis up on their sides. The edges grip the snow and hold you on the slope. [2K.2]

2K.1
KEEP YOUR SKIS ACROSS THE FALL LINE

2K.2
EDGE BY PUSHING YOUR KNEES UPHILL

You may also have trouble holding your skis straight. When you did pie turns you always kept part of your skis—either the tips or the tails—on the snow. As you get ready to sidestep, edge, and look uphill. [2L.1]

Stepping Out

Stand on your downhill ski, and lift the entire uphill ski off the snow. [2L.2]

Make sure your uphill ski is edged once you set it on the snow. Shift your weight on to it, then bring the downhill ski up to it—lifting the whole ski off the snow. [2L.3]

Now you can move your downhill pole up closer to you. [2L.4]

You will have to coordinate your hand and foot movements differently to keep from treading on your pole. Walking on the level, you said to yourself, "Opposite pole; opposite ski." When you sidestep, you must move your uphill pole out of the way as you first step up. [2L.2 again]

As you sidestep you can chant, "Same pole; same ski."

2L.4
*MOVE YOUR DOWNHILL
POLE UP*

2L.3
*BRING YOUR DOWNHILL
SKI UP*

2L.2
*LIFT YOUR WHOLE SKI OFF
THE SNOW*

2L.1
LOOK UPHILL

FALLING

All skiers fall. It's part of the sport. Even the best skiers believe, "If you never fall, you never learn." Obviously it's important to fall safely—without hurting yourself.

The trick is to keep from twisting anything as you fall. You will probably want to put your knee down first. Avoid that. *Don't* stick your knee in the snow. If you feel yourself falling, try to land on your hip, or better still, on your butt.

You can practice falling while you are sidestepping. Take your poles out of the snow, and let yourself fall uphill. [2M.1]

Fall onto the most padded part of your body. [2M.2]

2M.2
LAND CHEEKS FIRST

Class A: The Basics **29**

GETTING UP

Although it's difficult for some new skiers, standing up should not be a struggle. Knowing a few tricks makes it easy.

Take the pole straps off your wrists, and hold both poles together in front of you. Stick the tips in the snow just uphill from you. Grab the poles with your uphill hand—right above the baskets. Place your other hand at the tops of the poles. [2N.1]

Before you try to stand up, pull your feet up close to you.

You'll have trouble if you try to stand up all at once. Instead, keep your head down, your skis edged, and push off your uphill hand. [2N.2]

2N.1
MAKE SURE YOUR SKIS ARE
ACROSS THE FALL LINE

2N.2
BRING YOUR UPHILL FOOT
RIGHT UP UNDER YOUR BUTT

2N.3
PUSH UP

2N.4
ROLL OUT OVER YOUR SKIS

2N.5
THEN STAND UP AND START AGAIN

Move your hips out over your skis first. [2N.3]

Now you can get your balance, and straighten your legs. [2N.4] Put your poles back on, and get ready to sidestep some more. [2N.5]

Once you have a feel for tucking your feet under you, and rolling your weight out over your skis before you stand up, you won't need to take your poles off. Put your uphill hand on the snow, and push off it.

BULL-FIGHTER TURNS

You are about to actually ski for the first time. To get set up for a straight downhill run, you will do a *bull-fighter turn.* When you've done it, you will resemble the bull fighter known as a *picador,* the horseman who pricks the bull's neck with a lance. The bull-fighter turn is simply a matter of stepping into the fall line.

First, practice on the flat .

Sidestep until your instructor says, "Stop. That's high enough." You have reached a point on the slope from which you can safely glide to a stop on the natural run-out below. [2O.1]

Turn your upper body toward the fall line. Reach downhill with both poles and plant them firmly in the snow below you. Rest your hands on the tops of the poles, and straighten your arms to brace yourself. [2O.2]

Now make a pie turn. Turn your uphill ski first, leaving the tip on the snow. [2O.3] Then bring your downhill ski up to it.

Next, turn your downhill ski first, this time leaving the tail on the snow. [2O.4] Step the uphill ski over to the downhill ski. Keep taking little steps, always leaving part of the skis on the snow, so the skis don't cross.

Turn until you are facing right down the fall line. Look up. Now you're ready to ski. [2O.5]

2O.1
HANDS ON
POLE TOPS

2O.2
ARMS
STRAIGHT

2O.3
PIE TURN

2O.4
TAKE SMALL
STEPS

2O.5
LOOK WHERE
YOU'RE GOING

MILESTONE #1:
STRAIGHT RUNNING
AND STANCE

Your earliest straight runs should be done right in the fall line—perhaps in your instructor's tracks. Terrain selection is very important. Ideally you should ski down a very gentle incline, across a flat area, onto a slight uphill slope where you will come to a stop naturally. Your stance will determine how well this is done.

A good *stance* on skis is critical. Learn it now with straight runs. Some skiers never learn to stand correctly, and they suffer for it, always. Learn to stand properly on your skis from the very beginning.

Try to have what we call a *natural athletic stance.* Your instructor will help you find what stance works best for you. Practice on the flat first, so you know how it feels:

Feet

As you stand in the bull-fighter position adjust your feet. Imagine you are hanging by your arms from a horizontal bar. If you relaxed your legs while hanging, your feet would dangle directly below your hip sockets.

When you ski, your feet don't need to be close together. They also don't need to be far apart. They should be "open"—about hip-width apart. This is the most stable and workable position.

If you have wider hips, your feet will be farther apart. If you have narrower hips, your feet will be closer together. [2P.1]

Weight

To get started, release your arms, glide past your poles, picking them up as you go by. Hold the pole grips normally.

Feel the bottoms of your feet. Your weight should be on both feet more or less equally. [2P.2]

There is no need to stand on your toes; no need to stand on your heels. Feel as though you are standing on your whole foot. In other words, try to distribute your weight evenly, along the entire length of your skis. [2P.3]

Hands

Relax your arms, but don't ski as though you have your hands in your pockets. Spread your hands apart for extra balance.

Hold your hands more or less level, and high enough so your poles don't drag in the snow. Move your hands up, forward and into your field of vision. If you can see both hands out of the lower corners of your eyes, your hands are in a good position. [2P.4]

Joints

Non-skiers think the secret to skiing is, "Bend your knees." That's only partly correct. *All* joints must flex—equally. You should bend at the ankles. You should bend at the knees. You should bend at the hips. And your back should be slightly rounded. For you to be balanced and flexible, the angle at each joint should be about the same as the bend in the other joints. [2P.5]

Try to feel all this before you come to a stop. Sidestep uphill and ski again and again. Make lots of straight runs. Remember to look where you're going—not down at your feet or skis.

Of course you're going to be nervous. Sliding over snow seems weird at first, but there's nothing to be afraid of. The worst that can happen is that you fall, and you've already learned how to do that.

2P.5
FLEX ALL JOINTS EQUALLY

2P.1
STAND WITH FEET
HIP-WIDTH APART

2P.2
STAND ON BOTH FEET

2P.3
STAND IN THE MIDDLE
OF YOUR SKIS

2P.4
HOLD YOUR HANDS
READY—WHERE YOU CAN
SEE THEM

STRAIGHT-RUN EXPERIMENTS

There may be ten people in your class, all straight running with their eyes, feet, weight, hands and joints working "correctly." So why does everybody look a little bit different?

How you stand on skis depends on your height, your weight, your body type and the personal *style* you are already starting to develop.

Now it's time to experiment, approaching some extremes in stance, weighting and balancing.

Standing Low

How low can you go? See how close you can get to the ground before you start to lose your balance.

You will feel yourself weighting the tails of the skis more than the tips whenever you're too low. That's because your joints are now flexed unequally. You have more bend at the knees and hips than you do at the ankles. You're now at the limit of your shortness. Rise up slightly until you are balanced again.

Flex all joints equally, but be as short as you can be. Remember how this feels. [2Q]

Standing High

Stand up as tall as you can. When you're up this high it's difficult to balance. What's more, your joints start to lock up when they are so straight. You can't move freely.

At the limit of tallness, you are in a very precarious position. It's difficult to make balancing adjustments. Settle lower, so you're still relatively high but in balance. Remember how this feels too. [2R]

2R
STAND TALL, BUT BALANCED

2Q
STAND SHORT, BUT BALANCED

Standing Forward

In skiing we sometimes use the front (tip) portion of the ski. Sometimes we work the tail section. More on that later.

For now, experiment with forward lean. See how far forward you can go. You've gone too far when you feel you're no longer standing on your whole foot.

If your heels want to lift off your boot soles or you feel a great deal of pressure on your toes, you've probably reached the limits of forward lean.

Lean forward less, and put more weight on the whole length of your foot. Feel as though you're pressing your shin bone against the tongue of your boot. Then ask your muscles to remember how this feels. [2S]

Standing Aft

Lean back until you feel your toes lifting in the fronts of your boots. Do you feel you're going to tip over backward? If so, you've reached the extreme of backward leverage.

Bring your weight forward a little. Stand on your whole foot again with a little extra pressure on your heels. Remember how this feels. [2T]

Make sure you can always find *neutral,* as well as forward and back. Always be conscious of the soles of your feet. Also tune into the upper cuff of your boot, where it wraps around your ankle.

To get forward, feel pressure on the front of the cuff, near the boot tongue. To be aft on the skis, feel pressure on your heels. In neutral, you should feel no particular pressure from either boot cuff—on the fronts, backs or the sides of your ankles.

2S
PRESS FORWARD, BUT STAY BALANCED

2T
PRESS BACK, BUT STAY BALANCED

Stepping Experiment # 1

Like all other humans, you are a *biped,* a two-legged creature. That's why we use two skis. If we were four-legged animals, we'd need four.

Skiing is like walking. We step on one foot, then the other. Get used to the idea of standing on one ski, then the other. Ski in a neutral straight run. Gently shift your weight to one foot and find your balance there. [2U.1]

Lift the other foot off the snow, still balancing your weight on the ski that's on the snow. Put that raised ski down again and shift your weight to it. Lift the other ski off the snow. Repeat, as though you were walking down the hill. [2U.2]

Weight transfer from one foot to the other is fundamental to skiing.

2U.2
LIFT ONE SKI OFF THE SNOW

Stepping Experiment # 2

Sometimes we ski with our skis directly beneath us. When we do, the skis stay flat on the snow. On the other hand, we often ski with one or both of our skis out to one side, not under us. When this happens, the skis are tilted on edge. Play with that idea.

Take another straight run. Shift your weight to one ski and balance there. That's your "heavy" ski. [2V.1]

But instead of putting it right back down, move it sideways, away from the heavy ski. It's OK if the tail of the light ski seems to move further away than its tip does. It's perfectly normal to feel pigeon-toed. [2V.3]

When your feet are separated beyond the width of your hips, the skis ride on their inside edges. In other words, moving our feet out from under us edges our skis.

Transfer weight to the ski you just stepped, and make it heavy. Make the old ski light now, and move it over to your new heavy foot. [2V.4]

Then take a sideways step the other way, and step your feet back together.

2V.1
WEIGHT THE RIGHT SKI

2V.2
LIFT YOUR "LIGHT" SKI OFF THE SNOW

2V.3
STEP ONE FOOT TO THE SIDE

2V.4
STEP YOUR FEET BACK TOGETHER

MILESTONE # 2:
WEDGES

In a *wedge* the tips of your skis are together, and the tails apart. This is the most useful and practical stance in all of skiing. From the wedge you can make basic braking and turning maneuvers.

The wedge used to be called the *snowplow*. Whatever you call it, it has many benefits. First, the wide position of your feet gives you a very stable, broad base of support.

Second, because both feet are out from under you, both skis are on edge. The further your feet get from one another, the more the skis are edged.

Third, because the skis point toward each other, you have a ready-made turn in either direction already started for you. To put it another way, you have one ski that points to the left, and one that points to the right.

Some people advocate learning to ski without ever making a wedge. Don't buy that line of thinking. In a wedge, slowing down is just a matter of moving both tails out from under you more.

All of skiing is based on the wedge. If you can do a wedge, you have control. Master the wedge and skiing is easy.

Gliding Wedge

This involves a very narrow, pigeon-toed stance. Aside from the fact that your feet are apart and your toes are turned in, the gliding wedge is not much different from the straight run.

To understand how to make use of the gliding wedge, you should understand where most of your weight is centered. Regardless of your sex or your body type, your *center of mass,* as it's called, is located in the pelvic region, behind your belly button. Imagine it sitting, like a bowling ball, in your lower abdomen. [2W]

The more you move both feet out from under this bowling ball, the more the skis are tilted toward their edges. Move your feet out a little and the skis are only slightly edged.[2W again]

You can set up a gliding wedge while you are standing still in the bull-fighter stance. Hold yourself with your poles, spread the tails of the skis slightly, while you keep the tips together. Start skiing, weight both feet, and keep your leg joints flexed as you turn your feet toward each other.

As we've said, when you move your feet out from under your center of mass just a little, the skis are edged only a little. There's little friction in the

gliding wedge because the edges don't grab the snow very hard.

This means you don't slow down much. You glide instead. When we glide (and the skis are edged only slightly), it's very easy to turn our feet and skis.

2W
FEEL YOUR CENTER OF MASS

2X.1
TURN YOUR HEELS OUT
AND YOUR TOES IN

2X.2
EDGE MORE

2X.3
TURN YOUR
FEET MORE

2X.4
LET PRESSURE BUILD

The Braking Wedge

When we edge more, as in the braking wedge, it takes more effort to turn our feet. Here, we use all three of skiing's basic skills, edging, turning and pressuring. We move our feet further out from under our center of mass, and *edge* more as a result. Because our feet are further apart, we must *turn* them in on each other more to hold the wedge.

The combination of turning and edging, makes the edges grip more. We exert more *pressure* on a smaller area—the narrow edge of the running surface, instead of the whole ski base.

The added pressure creates resistance, slowing us down. Gravity still wants to pull us down the hill, but friction holds us back. The more friction we generate by edging and turning our feet, the more snow we push away from our edges. The more we "plow" the snow, the more pressure we feel.

To go from a gliding wedge [2X.1] to a braking wedge,

Keep your weight on both feet, and widen your stance to get more edge. [2X.2]

As your feet go further apart, turn both feet toward each other more and stay balanced along the length of both skis. [2X.3]

Create still more friction by edging and turning more. Stay balanced in the middle of each ski. As resistance builds, you will feel you are pressing your edges deeper into the snow. [2X.4]

You will go slower and slower. Eventually a braking wedge results in a stop. Notice that as you slow down your center of mass sinks lower and lower—closer to the snow. Later we will refer to this lowering as "down motion."

In a braking wedge you should feel no particular strain, and no pain. If you hurt, particularly in the hip socket, you are somehow out of balance. Ease your weight forward, or back, until it doesn't hurt anymore.

Class A: The Basics **39**

Wedge Turns

To make a wedge turn, put the skills you already know to work for you. First you will use the *turning* skill, then *edging,* then *pressuring.* Make your first turns on a very flat slope.

To help you feel what's happening, say to yourself, "Foot . . . leg . . . knee." At the start of a wedge turn you must turn your foot. In the middle of the turn you will use your whole leg to help you edge. At the end of the turn your knee will help you press the ski into the snow. Repeat: "Foot . . . leg . . . knee."

Let's break this down into *foot turns, leg turns* and *knee turns.* in a narrow, gliding wedge your skis are edged only slightly. This makes them very easy to turn. Remember that whenever your tips are together and your tails are apart, you always have a ski that points left, and one that points right. [2Y.1]

Even before you learned to sidestep you learned to pick one ski off the snow and turn it in either direction. Now that movement comes into play, except this time you'll be in motion and both skis will be on the snow. You are simply going to twist your feet inside your boots.

2Y.1
WEDGE

In skiing we don't lean the way we want to go, as we would on a bicycle, we turn the *outside* ski (in the case of a wedge turn, the one that points where we wish to go). Keep turning your outside foot. [2Y.2]

There is no need to twist your body in any way. Keep your leg joints flexed, and hold both hands where you can see them.

Make lots of foot turns.

2Y.2
*TURN YOUR FEET THE WAY
YOU WANT TO GO*

2Y.3
TURN THE OUTSIDE FOOT

2Z.1
TURN THE FOOT

2Z.2
THEN TURN YOUR LEG FOR EDGE

Next, are the leg turns. A foot turn takes a long time to accomplish because it's done so subtly. If we add more muscle power, we can make a tighter turn.

Ski in a fairly narrow wedge so the skis are flat and easy to turn. Again, turn the foot on the ski that's already pointing where you want to go. This gets the turn started. [2Z.1]

Make lots of foot turns. As you begin to change direction with your foot, rotate your whole leg. Feel all the big muscles above your knee turning together. This widens the wedge and gives you more edge. [2Z.2]

Added power from the thigh muscles will make this turn sharper, so much so that you feel more weight on your outside ski. That's as it should be. Stay balanced on the middle of that ski. [2Z.3]

Make lots of "foot-leg" turns.

2Z.3
FEEL WEIGHT BUILD ON YOUR OUTSIDE SKI

Class A: The Basics **41**

2AA.1
TWIST YOUR FOOT

2AA.2
TURN YOUR LEG, AND FLEX YOUR KNEE

Now let's add the final ingredient—pressure in knee turns. We already discovered that a sharper turn forces more weight to our working outside ski. (It's the same *centrifugal force* passengers feels in a car when they're pushed against the door during a turn.) In skiing we can use this extra force.

Start your turn as before, by twisting your foot, then turning the leg for more edge. [2AA.1]

With more edge on the outside ski, and more friction, the ski turns sharply, and gets "heavier" as your weight is pushed toward it. Add to that heaviness by pushing your knee forward, in the direction of the turn. [2AA.2]

Keep flexing your knee for more pressure. The natural forces of the turn, plus your muscle power, actually cause the ski to bend. With all this pressure the ski's edge slices into the snow, giving you all kinds of control. [2AA.3]

Make lots of "foot-leg-knee" turns.

2AA.3
ADD PRESSURE

MILESTONE # 3:
LINKED WEDGE TURNS

Obviously, skiing is not a matter of making one turn at a time. We make turns in sequence, linking one turn to the next. Once you link turns, you're really skiing.

When we glide in a wedge, we tend to stand quite high on our skis. As we turn the foot on the ski that's pointing where we want to go, then turn the leg to edge, and flex the knee to press, we tend to lower our center of mass (the "bowling ball"). At the end of a turn, as we flex our legs more, we show *down motion.*

We can't keep going down, and down, and down. So the down motion that ends the first turn must become *up motion* to begin the next, as shown on the following two pages.

Stand very high. [2BB.1]

Turn the foot . . . .[2BB.2]

Then the leg . . . .[2BB.3]

And gently flex the knee. [2BB.4] Now you are quite low.

Stand taller again so you can go down through the next turn. [2BB.5]

Turn the foot . . . .[2BB.6]

Then the leg . . . .[2BB.7]

And flex the knee. [2BB.8]

By completing a wedge turn, you will steer way out of the fall line and come to a stop. This is a lot easier than stopping in a straight braking wedge. [2BB.9]

Remember this new chant for wedge turns, "Foot . . . leg . . . knee . . . (Rise up) . . . "

Believe it or not, you may have tried all this by the end of Class A. Of course, your wedges and turns will be far from perfect.

You may also learn to ride a surface lift that pulls you up the hill, or even learn to ride a small chairlift that actually lifts you off the ground.

Practice and rest before the next class.

2BB.1
STAND HIGH

2BB.2
TURN FOOT

2BB.3
TURN LEG

2BB.4
FLEX KNEE

2BB.9
STOP

44   *Class A: The Basics*

2BB.5
GET TALL

2BB.6
TURN FOOT

2BB.7
TURN LEG

2BB.8
FLEX KNEE

CLASS B

To begin your second lesson, Class B, you should again be ready for line-up at the ski school meeting place.

If you took Class A in the morning, and are taking an afternoon session, you might have the same instructor, and may join the same group you were in this morning. But you also might be in a new class.

By now you can be expected to put on your skis and your poles by yourself. But if you need a reminder, don't be afraid to ask for help. In either case, an instructor will give everyone a quick equipment check.

A teacher will then move your group away from the ski school meeting place. If new people have joined ski school, one or more instructors might ask you to ride a short lift (or even sidestep uphill) for what's called a *ski-off.*

RIDING A LIFT

If you have never ridden a ski lift before, you might be intimidated at first. There is nothing to be afraid of. Getting transported up the hill is easier than riding a merry-go-round.

Basically there are two types of lifts: 1) *aerial lifts,* like chairlifts, gondolas and trams, which actually lift you off the ground, and 2) *surface lifts* which pull you over the snow on your skis. It's easy to understand why surface lifts are sometimes called "tows."

Gondolas and trams are the easiest to ride. You take your skis off while the lift is stopped, stand or sit inside, and ride to the top. The lift stops, you get out and put your skis on again. It's like an elevator.

Chairlifts

Riding a chairlift, which keeps moving, is more like riding an escalator. You keep your skis on. Chairlifts are designed for one person, two people (double chairs), three people (triples), and even four people (quads).

Your instructor will give you a briefing beforehand. You'll be told to take your pole straps off and hold both poles in your outside hand. When it's your turn to load, you'll ski into a flat, specially-prepared loading area, and stop in a specific spot.

Turn and look behind you. (On some chairs you turn toward your partner(s); on some you turn away from them. If it's a triple, and you happen to be in the middle, turn either way.)

The chair will come up behind you. Just sit down as the attendant loads you gently into the chair. It will swoop you off your feet and into the air. Relax and enjoy the ride.

When you near the top, the ground will come up to meet you. Keep your ski tips up so they don't catch in the snow. The off-loading point will be easy to see.

When you get there stand up, keeping your skis pointed straight ahead, and ski down the ramp. There is no need to do a wedge or to turn on the unloading ramp. Below there will be plenty of room to stop.

Remember: if you have difficulty at any time during loading or unloading, the operator will stop the chairlift immediately.

Advanced Wedge Turns & Basic Christies

Surface Lifts

Rope tows, T-bars, platter lifts, and J-bars are the most common surface lifts. The only trick to riding them is *not* to sit down.

Some rope tows have handles; some do not. Line your skis up in the track parallel to the tow rope, turn and wait for a handle to come by. Flex your knees, grasp the handle, and let it pull you up the hill.

If there are no handles, you will hang onto the rope itself. Grip the rope slowly, letting it slip through your fingers at first. (If you try to grip it all at once, it may jerk you off your feet.)

Some people like to ride a gripless rope tow with both hands in front of them. Others are more comfortable with one hand in front, and one behind them. Let go of the rope at the top.

A T-bar is an upside-down T suspended from a moving cable. It pulls two people at once. A J-bar (which could just as easily be called an L-bar) and a platter lift each tow one skier.

Stand straight in the track at the loading area. The attendant will slip the bar under your butt, or a round disk (platter) between your legs. Your immediate reaction may be to sit on it. Resist that urge or you will fall down.

Instead, flex your knees a little, and stand up, letting the bar pull you up the hill. Keep your skis in the prepared track and enjoy the ride.

Near the top, the track may turn away from the lift at a slight angle. The track will also slope gently downhill. This is the unloading area. Push the bar away from you and ski down the ramp, stopping below.

All classes above Class A usually begin with a ski-off and a *split.* At the top of an easy hill one instructor will say, "Please ski down this hill making the best turns, or wedges, you can. Stop below the other instructor at the bottom."

Another instructor will watch you ski, and split the larger group into smaller classes according to each student's experience level. Instructors watch ski-offs and do splits several times a day, so they get very good at it.

They will place people properly 98% of the time—even after seeing them make only a few turns. Once in a while the split instructor will miss, in which case the instructor assigned to the class will soon notice the mistake and move the misplaced student to a more appropriate class.

After the split, chances are good you will *not* wind up in the same group with your spouse, family, or friends. Expect this. It's probably for the best.

HOW AND WHY SKIS TURN

A ski turns, first because of the way it is shaped and second because it is flexible enough to bend.

Look more closely at your ski. It is shaped roughly like a greatly-elongated hour glass. The ski is widest near its tip, narrowest near its middle, and wide again at the tail. The narrowest part of the ski is called the *waist*. When your foot is in the binding, the waist is right under your heel.

The part of the ski between the toe piece of the binding and the tip is called the *shovel*. The shovel is actually wider than the tail, which is of course wider than the waist. The widest part of any ski is at the shovel.

When you look closely at the sidewall of any ski, you'll see that it's not straight. It curves because the ski's width changes from widest at the shovel, narrowest at the waist, and wider at the tail. This interior curve along a ski's sidewall is called *sidecut*.

Sidecuts vary a tiny bit between various models of skis, but all skis have sidecut. It's this sidecut and flex that give a ski its turning properties.

When you place a ski on the snow, base down, the shovel will rest on the snow, the tail will rest on the snow, but the waist of the ski will be a little elevated—off the snow. Like a natural arch the ski's center bends upward, ever so slightly. This arch is built into the ski on purpose. It's called *camber*.

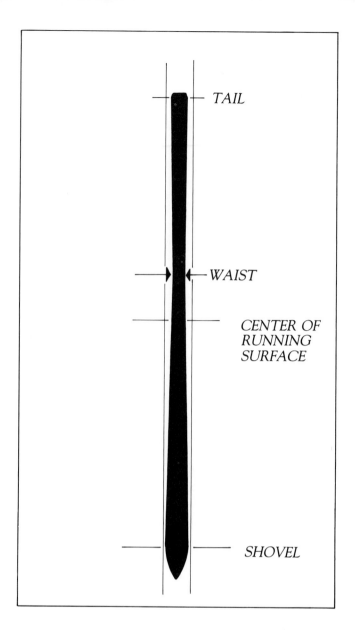

TAIL

WAIST

CENTER OF RUNNING SURFACE

SHOVEL

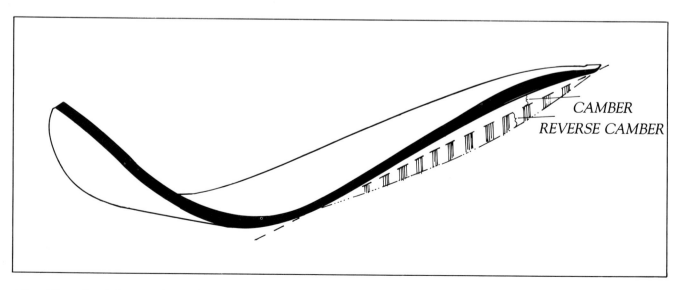

CAMBER
REVERSE CAMBER

When you step into the binding, the camber disappears as your body weight presses down on the ski. If the ski had no camber, your weight would press the waist of the ski into the snow so far that the ski would be shaped like a very flat U. That would be bad. Camber distributes your weight evenly.

When the ski is tipped toward its edge, on the other hand, and pressure is applied, a ski will bend into the very flat U just mentioned. In other words, the camber has been flattened out, and the ski is bent further still. That's good. In this case, we say the ski has been flexed into *reverse camber.*

The fact that a ski can bend toward reverse camber also helps us change direction. Reverse camber and sidecut operate as a team to help us turn.

SKI BENT INTO REVERSE CAMBER

There's one more factor to consider: the ski boot. The boot is designed to give us *leverage*. That's why it's so high, and so stiff, and why it should fit so snugly. It's a fulcrum—a means of exerting pressure.

If we push against the sides of the boot with our ankle bone—when we're sidestepping, for example—that push is communicated to the ski, and the ski is levered onto its edge.

When we twist our foot inside the boot, that rotary force reaches the ski through our boot, giving the ski turning impetus.

If we push against the tongue at the front of the boot, we apply more pressure to the ski's tip. When we stand more on our heel, we apply leverage through the boot, pressuring the tail of the ski.

We use different parts of the ski at different times for different reasons. We ride flat on the base when we want speed. We edge when we want to create friction. We use the front part of the ski when we want to turn sharply and brake. We use the back part of the ski for longer, more leisurely turns.

The best place to turn a ski is from its middle. That's because the sidecut places the waist right under your heel, as we've already mentioned. Your foot is right at the center of the sidecut's interior curve, and we can move weight forward or back from this neutral, centered position.

What's more, from its middle it's easy to lever the ski onto its edge through the fulcrum of the boot by pressing against the inside of the boot cuff. It's easiest to apply torque, or turning force, from the ski's middle.

It's also easy to bend the whole ski evenly—into reverse camber. With your weight in the middle

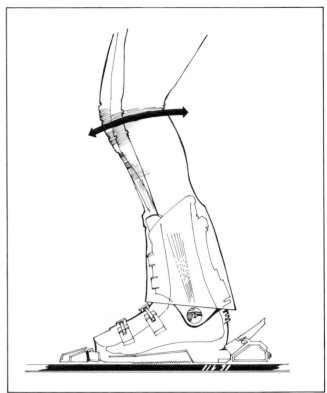

LEVERING ACTION

WEIGHT IN THE MIDDLE OF SKIS

of the ski, a nice, even bend usually permits the ski to turn with just the right amount of skid. Reason? The whole edge can work in the snow.

If we push against the front part of the ski and edge at the same time, the edge at the widest part of the ski (the shovel) will engage the snow first, creating a lot of friction there. This causes the front part of the ski to slow down.

If we add some turning force to this forward leverage, the tip of the ski grabs the snow. But the tail, obviously connected to the tip, is released because there's no pressure on it. So the tip slows down and the tail, because it has farther to travel in the turn, speeds up, and *skids* around the corner.

That's why we make sharp turns when we lever forward. Making a turn with just the right arc is a matter of controlling the amount of skid at the ski's tail.

Remember that sidecut makes the ski widest at the shovel, and not quite so wide at the tail. Also keep in mind that a ski flexes more easily at the tip that it does at the tail. When we apply pressure to the tail we have (1) less sidecut to work with, and (2) less flex.

It is harder to bend the tail section into reverse camber than it is to bend the tip. That's why we can only make longer arced turns with the tail.

A SHARP TURN BY LEVERING FORWARD
(Below-the-snow view)

CONTROLLING SPEED

We make wedges and turns for one main reason: to regulate speed. We resist gravity, which always wants us to speed up, by widening the wedge or by making sharp turns.

When the wedge widens, we create more friction at our edges and slow down. When we turn, we steer ourselves out of the fall line—away from gravity's grip. If we don't turn, but *stay* in the fall line for too long, we run the risk of losing control.

Wedge Change-ups

The *wedge change-up* is a series of slowing and going movements. It's a speed-control exercise using the straight wedge. It also teaches us about "up" movement and "down" movement.

Start out in a wide braking wedge, with your feet far out from under you and the skis edged a lot. With your skis turned in this much, and your feet this far apart, you will ski very slowly. Your center of mass will also be low. [3A.1 and 3A.2]

When you get taller, the wedge gets narrower as your feet move beneath you. You accelerate. [3A.3]

You have gone from a braking wedge to a gliding wedge. [3A.4]

Settle lower, back into a braking wedge, and feel the deceleration. [3A.5]

Continue this way of slowing down and speeding up until you run out of hill.

3A.1
SINK

3A.2
RISE

3A.3
LET GO

3A.4
GLIDE

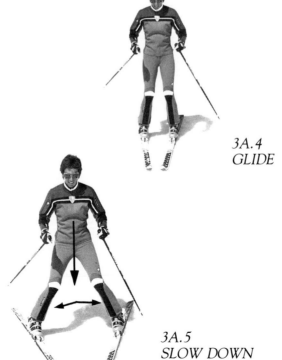

3A.5
SLOW DOWN

3B.1
WEIGHT YOUR OUTSIDE SKI

3B.2
FOOT . . .

Foot-Leg-Knee and Weight Transfer

Skiing is a matter of slowing down, letting go, slowing down, then letting go again. Generally, when we come up, we release pressure on our edges and let our skis go. By the same token, when we slow down, the result is down motion. We associate "up" with going; "down" with slowing.

Practice making linked wedge turns. Shift your weight from one ski to the other as you turn. You are always turning the outside ski, the ski that's about to become your downhill ski.

As you complete one turn, flexing your knee, you will have turned out of the fall line and slowed down. Press on the inside edge of your outside ski; you will be low. [3B.1]

Let go of the first turn by rising up. Neutralize your weight by standing on both skis. Your wedge may narrow. Turn the new outside foot. [3B.2]

Turn your outside leg to add edge. [3B.3]

Flex the knee forward to increase pressure on the new outside ski. Actively transfer some more weight to that ski to increase the pressure on it. Now that ski is "heavy." [3B.4]

Turns result when you apply a combination of *rotary forces* (turning), edging, and pressure. Pressure results from the natural centrifugal force that forces your weight to the outside of any turn, as well as active weight transfer.

Whenever we transfer weight and press an edge into the snow, we build friction and slow down. As we slow down we go lower. To speed up we must rise. We "slow" whenever we turn out of the fall line. We "go" whenever we turn toward the fall line, where gravity can pull on us harder if friction is diminished.

3B.3
LEG . . .

3B.4
KNEE

Class B: Advanced Wedge Turns & Basic Christies **53**

For the most part, turning toward the fall line is easy since gravity is working for us. Turning out of the fall line is the hard part. It requires more effort because gravity is working against us. Our only ally is friction.

Remember these things. They apply to almost all skiing turns.

Pressing On The Ski Front

While you are turning, and without overdoing it, get to know the front part of your ski. You'll discover that it responds quite differently than the tail.

Without getting out of balance, press your shin bone into the tongue of your boot. Turn your foot. [3C.1]

Turn your leg, still levering against the forebody (front) of the ski. [3C.2]

Keep turning, flexing the knee forward still more. [3C.3]

Complete the turn by coming to a full stop. [3C.4]

You will have made a very tight turn—perhaps too tight. A ski turns more quickly when you apply a lot of edge and pressure to its front.

When slopes get steeper, we need to make tighter turns because we want to spend less time in the fall line. So we tend to bring our weight forward and lower our center of mass when it's steep.

3C.1
PRESS FORWARD

3C.2
APPLY ROTARY FORCE

3C.3
WEIGHT THE OUTSIDE SKI

3C.4
STOP

3D.1
*PRESS THROUGH YOUR
HEEL*

3D.2
USE ROTARY FORCE

3D.3
SHIFT WEIGHT

Pressing On The Ski Tail

Now see what happens when you turn by putting more pressure on the tail of the ski. Feel as though you are pushing down, through the heel of your outside foot.

Weight your heel, and turn the foot. [3D.1]

Turn the leg, still pressing on the heel of your outside foot. [3D.2]

Transfer your weight . . . .[3D.3]

And flex the knee. [3D.4]

Notice how much longer it takes you to finish a turn when your weight is further back. The arc or the turn is also longer, more stretched out. In fact, you may have trouble coming to a stop at all. The skis want to keep going.

By pressing back, we have somewhat less control. We can afford to make such long, relaxed turns only on flat, wide-open slopes. Yet at a very advanced level, tail pressure has its advantages. More on that later.

3D.4
FLEX KNEE

Class B: Advanced Wedge Turns & Basic Christies **55**

Pressing On The Ski Middle

For most skiing turns, we avoid the extremes of front and back by standing right over the mid-section of the ski. This way, we try to distribute weight and pressure along the ski's entire running surface.

Practice some more wedge turns by centering your weight on the outside ski. At least 90% of all the wedge turns you will need to make should look like this:

Start each turn by standing high in a gliding wedge. Turn the foot. [3E.1]

Edge with the leg. [3E.2]

Transfer weight and flex the knee. [3E.3]

Balance over the middle of the outside ski—the ski that has just become the downhill ski. [3E.4]

3E.1
GLIDE

3E.2
EDGE

3E.4
WEIGHT THE DOWNHILL SKI

3E.3
PRESSURE THE OUTSIDE SKI

Overedging

It's possible to edge too much, too soon. This can cause a problem. If you tilt a ski too high on its side, it can't bend. What's more, its sidecut can't work. So the ski wants to run straight. This is called *edgelock,* and it's a common problem for beginners who are just learning to edge.

Look at Jerry. He has over edged and is edgelocked. [3F] See how his hips are out of whack—way off center. His center of mass is right over one ski so that ski is flat. The other is overedged because it's so far out from under him.

To correct the problem he merely has to move his hips back toward the middle of his wedge. He has to move his center of mass *between* the skis. You want to keep your hips "inside" your wedge.

3F
EDGELOCK

MILESTONE #4:
TRAVERSING

Holding a wedge all the time can be tiring. It's also unnecessary. As we ski across the fall line for any distance, we can leave the wedge for a while and let our skis run more or less in the same direction. When we do this, we *traverse*.

Traversing allows us two things. First, it lets us rest without building up too much speed, such as when we straight run. Second, it gives us a chance to get organized for the upcoming turn.

It's best to practice traverses on a wide, fairly flat slope. Traverses are much like straight runs, except you're skiing across, rather than directly down the hill.

There are two types of traverses—*slipping traverses,* and *holding traverses.* Both are useful at different times. Neither is better nor worse than the other.

Slipping Traverses

This occurs when we move across and, to a lesser extent, down the slope. Our feet should be about hip-width apart, our weight should be balanced on the middle of the skis, all joints should be flexed, and our hands should be forward where we can see them. [3G.1]

Because we are on a slope, traversing is a little like walking down the street with one foot on the curb and one foot in the gutter. One foot is higher than the other, and our hips tilt as a result. We have to adjust our bodies to this *pelvic tilt.*

To be most comfortable in a traverse, lead with your uphill ski by about half a boot length. Your whole body will turn slightly toward the valley, meaning that your uphill knee, hip and shoulder will also lead—by about the same amount. [3G.2]

Edge enough to keep from slipping sideways completely, but not so much that you make a perfectly straight track across the slope. This is, after all a slipping traverse. The slipping slows your forward movement, by the way. [3G.3]

Some skiers find a slipping traverse to be most natural.

*3G.1
NATURAL ATHLETIC
STANCE*

*3G.2
LEAD WITH YOUR UPHILL
SIDE*

*3G.3
EDGE A LITTLE*

3H.3
*WEIGHT ON THE DOWNHILL
SKI*

3H.2
*LEAD WITH YOUR UPHILL
SIDE*

3H.1
EDGE MORE TO HOLD

Holding Traverses

These are much the same. This time, though, push your knees and hip further into the hill (as you did while sidestepping), so the skis are edged more.

This time the objective is to ski from Point A to Point B on the other side of the slope without drifting sideways. [3H.1]

Again you'll be in the basic straight-running stance, except that you'll lead with the uphill foot, knee, hip and shoulder. [3H.2]

Try to hold your edge as you traverse. Notice how you can almost read the lettering on the base of Carol's ski. That tells us she has her ski high on its edge. You will find it easiest to hold an edge if you stand with more of your weight on the lower ski. [3H.3]

Some skiers find a holding traverse to be more natural. Learn both.

To stop at the end of any traverse you can do a braking wedge, a wedge turn, or step your skis uphill—as though doing a moving sidestep.

In the same way that rules are meant to be broken, traverses are meant to be eliminated, but over time. They allow us to cross a slope in control, and they allow us a "position" to return to between turns. In that way they let us get balanced and organized for what is going to happen shortly.

But the term *position* implies something static—a pose. Posing is something to avoid in skiing. Good skiers have learned new turns by beginning and ending them in traverses. Once the turn is learned, the turns should be connected and the traverses thrown out.

It's a mistake to get so good at traversing that you neglect your turns. Skiing is movement. We move in and out of turns, not in and out of traverses.

CHRISTIES

Any skidded turn is called a *christy*. All christies are considered more advanced than wedge turns.

Traverse Sideslips

To make a skidded christy we have to know how to release an edge, and how to get it back again. Because a skid is sliding plus slipping, to skid we must first learn to slip. We can do this by going from a holding traverse, to slipping traverse, and back to a holding traverse.

In a holding traverse our knees and hips are pushed into the hill to create edge. Whenever we bend our knees this much, we are in a relatively low stance on our skis. [31.1]

If we rise, the angle at our knee joint starts to disappear. The knees are pushed into the hill less, the skis are flattened, and the edges are released. We begin to slip. [31.2]

You can practice this while you are standing still. Then try it while you're moving. As you are learning, your instructor might take you by the hands and pull you sideways gently, to let you feel the slip.

31.1
DOWN TO HOLD AN EDGE

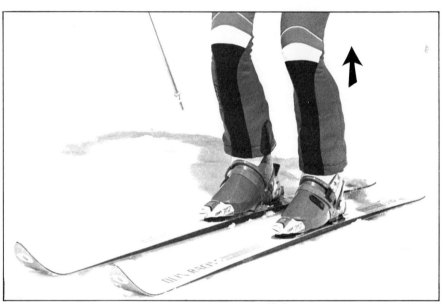

31.2
UP TO RELEASE AN EDGE

SOME TERMINOLOGY

Before we go too much further, we need to get some terms straight. The words sliding, slipping, *and* skidding *sometimes confuse skiers because often they're used incorrectly. Each means something different, as follows:*
Sliding—*Skis slide when they are moving straight ahead—either flat or on edge. When we make a straight run our skis are sliding because they are going where the tips are pointing. When we do a holding traverse, our skis are also sliding.*
Slipping—*Skis are slipping when they are moving sideways. If our tips are pointing across the hill, but our movement is downhill, we are slipping, as in a slipping traverse. We*

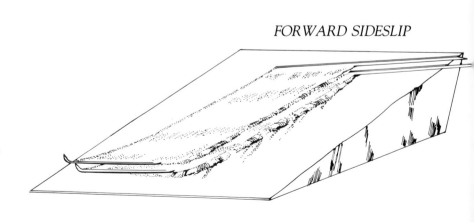

FORWARD SIDESLIP

The traverse sideslip teaches us about controlling our skis when they are drifting sideways. *Sideslipping*, remember, offers a useful way to slow down—without using a wedge.

Start out in a low, holding traverse, with your knees pushed into the hill. [3J.1]

Gradually stand up . . . [3J.2]

As your legs extend, the edges will release. [3J.3] Don't come up so high that your knees lock. Never straighten your legs completely.

When your edges no longer hold, gravity wants to pull you sideways. It may feel strange. To resist the sideways pull, you'll be tempted to contort your body in some way.

Change nothing. Try not to shift your weight from your downhill ski to your uphill ski. Try not to turn your body in any way. Try not to press forward or back. [3J.4]

Gently settle back down to a holding traverse. You knees will go back into the hill, engaging the edges, and slowing the slip. [3J.5]

Traverse straight ahead, with your edges holding. [3J.6]

During a traverse sideslip you will feel most secure when you're on your edges, least secure during the slipping phase. It's important to learn how to balance when your edges are released.

Stand in the middle of your skis. If you lean forward when your edges are not holding, the tips will turn downhill toward the fall line. If you weight your heels, the tails will slip downhill faster than the tips. Either is awkward.

3J.1
STAND LOW

3J.2
RISE UP

3J.3
NEVER LOCK
YOUR KNEES

3J.4
DON'T CHANGE
A THING

3J.5
HOLD A GOOD TRAVERSE

3J.6
EDGE AGAIN

can only slip downhill, of course. When we slip more downhill than across the hill, we are said to be sideslipping.

Skidding—A skid is a combination of sliding and slipping. Because skidding involves both forward and sideways movement, a skid usually leaves a wide, curved track in the snow. Normally, as we learned earlier, the tail of the ski skids more than the tip of a ski as it takes this arc-shaped path.

Most turns beyond the wedge turn are round, skidded turns. Skidding feels odd at first, and learning to do it well takes time. Asking a novice skier to skid is like asking the average driver to drive into a four-wheel drift.

3K.1
TRAVERSE

3K.2
UP TO WEDGE

3K.3
ROTARY

3K.4
EDGE

3K.5
PRESS

3K.6
STOP TURNING

3K.7
TRAVERSE

Linking Traverses and Wedge Turns

Let's connect two traverses with a wedge turn.
Begin with a traverse. This is resting time. [3K.1]
Rise to a wedge. [3K.2]
Turn the foot. [3K.3]
Transfer weight and turn the the whole leg to give
you more edge. [3K.4]
Flex the outside knee to add pressure. [3K.5]
Relax your inside (uphill) leg . . . [3K.6]
And let your skis run together. You are now back
in a traverse. Now you can rest again. Look ahead
toward the next turn. [3K.7]

Link lots to traverses and wedge turns, following in
your instructor's tracks. As you get better and better
at this, your teacher may ski a bit faster. Keep up.

3L.1
TRAVERSE

3L.2
GLIDE

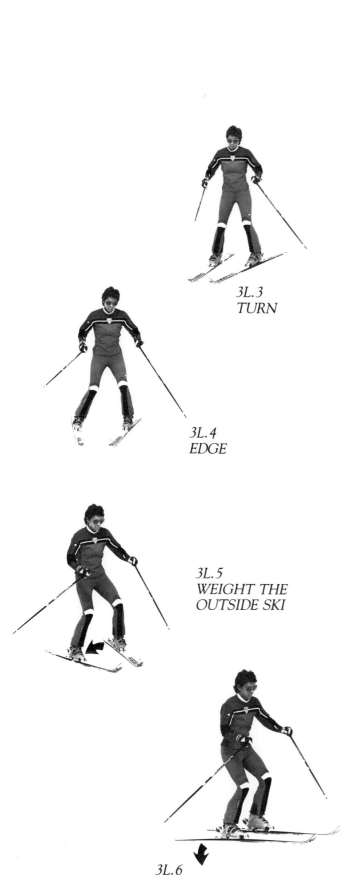

3L.3
TURN

3L.4
EDGE

3L.5
WEIGHT THE
OUTSIDE SKI

Spontaneous Christies

After some mileage you might do a skidded turn on your own—without a lot of prompting. We could call this a *spontaneous christy.* The key ingredients are confidence and more speed. A spontaneous christy might happen like this:

From a rapid traverse . . .[3L.1]

Rise to a narrow, gliding wedge. [3L.2]

Turn the foot. [3L.3]

Turn the leg for edge [3L.4]

Here's the interesting part. As you flex the knee, the pressure created by edging, plus centrifugal force, makes the outside ski bend. The bending ski is out from under you—edged and heavy. The inside ski is beneath you—flat and light. [3L.5]

The light inside ski, because it's so flat, may naturally slide over to the outside ski. The outside ski will skid at the same time. [3L.6]

Now your skis are pointing in the same direction. You've just made a skidded turn. Start a new traverse. [3L.7]

Not everyone will make a christy this spontaneously. If you don't, worry not. There are other ways to get you there.

3L.6
SKID

3L.7
TRAVERSE AGAIN

3M.1
WEDGE

3M.2
MATCH . . .

Wedge Skids

Whenever we bring our skis from a tips-together, tails-apart wedge into a parallel relationship we *match* our skis. Matching helps us skid.

Ski across the slope in a wedge, with most of your weight on your downhill ski. Your traverse should be pretty steep—close to the fall line. Stand tall. [3M.1]

Your uphill ski will feel light, because you have so little weight on it. Brush the tail of your uphill ski toward the tail of the downhill ski by pivoting your foot. This is matching. [3M.2]

Because you are standing over a fairly flat downhill ski, the matching movement causes both skis to skid in unison. The tails skid further downhill than the tips, and now both skis point more out of the fall line—toward a flatter traverse. [3M.3]

Make lots of wedge skids, in both directions.

3M.3
AND SKID

3N.1
TRAVERSE

3N.2
WEDGE

Start, as usual, in a short traverse. [3N.1]

Open to a wedge. [3N.2]

Turn the foot. [3N.3]

Turn the upper leg, and transfer weight. [3N.4]

Flex the outside knee. [3N.5]

Be patient. Don't be in a big rush to match.

Come all the way through your wedge turn until your inside ski is flat. Now you can match—when the turn is nearly completed. [3N.6]

3N.3
TURN

MILESTONE #5: BASIC CHRISTY

The *basic christy* is just what its name suggests—basically a wedge turn with a match and skid at its bottom end. It's like the wedge skid, except this time you're going to cross the fall line.

Basic christies mark the end of every skier's novice stage. If you can make a basic christy, it's time to call yourself an intermediate.

3N.4
SHIFT WEIGHT

3N.5
PRESS

3N.6
WAIT

Matching will help you skid. The skid may be brief, but it sets up both skis for a nice, flat traverse. [3N.7]

Traverse toward your next turn and start all over again. Wedge . . . turn . . . wait . . . match . . . skid.

At the end of Class B you should be making sound basic christies. The last half hour of the lesson may be spent skiing in line behind your instructor and the other members of your class.

3N.7
MATCH . . .
AND SKID

Ski teachers may seem to have eyes in the back of their heads as they lead you. They will see you make mistakes and will offer corrections and other suggestions. Instructors should let you know what you're doing right, as well as what you could be doing better.

This would be a good time to stay out of class for a day, or at least part of a day. It's also be a very *bad* time to accept a lot of advice from family, friends, or other "good" skiers.

Ski with your friends for a while, have lunch with your friends, above all, have fun with your friends. But discourage impromptu coaching meant to help you keep up with them on harder slopes. Excuse yourself and practice what your instructor has taught you.

Your goals should be:
1) To ski faster and with more confidence.
2) To be in total balance at all times—during and between turns.
3) To match earlier in your turns.
4) To skid through a larger portion of the turn.
5) To shorten the length of your traverses.

Get to work. You have a lot to accomplish before Class C.

SOME WORDS ON SAFETY

While you're practicing, you have time to take a few deep breaths and think about the freedom of skiing. As in everything else, "freedom" involves certain responsibilities.

You're not on the "big" mountain yet, but you're moving off the easiest "baby" slopes, gradually working your way into the "fast lane." It's time to start thinking about making skiing as safe as possible, both for yourself and others.

We often compare skiing to driving. That's because skiers, like cars, are moving quickly in more or less the same direction—downhill. As on the highway, there are certain "rules of the road" that must be observed. Remember:

● Ski in control. Always be sure you can stop and avoid other skiers and the fixed objects (trees, rocks, etc.) that exist in every ski area.

● When you overtake another skier from behind, you are responsible for passing her properly. She has the right of way. If the other skier suddenly changes direction, it's up to you to avoid a collision.

● Whether you're skiing in a class or alone, you must avoid stopping in a place that obstructs the trail for other skiers. It's also a bad idea to stop in any spot where you can't be seen from above. By the same token, be cautious when you can't see what's happening below you. As you ski over terrain that blocks the view below, use caution. A child, a friend, or a less capable skier may have fallen there. Make sure you can ski around someone who is down.

• After any reststop at the side of a trail, look uphill before starting out into traffic again. Use the same caution you would use crossing a busy street.

• Ski trails often merge, just like highways. Watch out for, and yield to, other skiers in these high-traffic zones.

• Like most skiers you are probably a bit adventurous, curious, free-spirited and anxious to find the best snow to ski on. Don't let these character traits lure you into places or trails that are closed. Areas that are closed (either temporarily or permanently) are closed for safety.

• Make sure to wear retention straps or ski brakes which prevent runaway skis.

• Don't get cocky. Ski only as fast as conditions and your ability permit. Slopes can be specially groomed for our enjoyment, but mountains exist in a world controlled more by Mother Nature than by people and machines. Wind, sun, temperature changes, and new snow alter this environment constantly, making it impossible to remove every natural obstacle. Stay alert!

BE AWARE. SKI WITH CARE.

Intermediate Christies

Has your practice paid off? At the ski-off for Class C, your basic christies should look something like this:

♦ Are you comfortable and balanced in a traverse? Do your hands appear to be ready? Can you carry a little more speed [4A.1]?

♦ Can you rise easily to a gliding wedge [4A.2]?

♦ Do you begin to steer toward the fall line by turning your outside foot [4A.3]?

♦ Do you show strong rotary (turning) ability? Do you transfer weight to the outside ski [4A.4]?

♦ Can you match your skis shortly after you cross the fall line [4A.5]?

♦ Can can you skid both skis from the matching point all the way to the new traverse line [4A.6]?

These are some of the things that the instructor who splits the classes will be looking for.

During the first part of Class C, you might think that nothing new is being introduced. But you should realize that the terrain you are skiing on is changing. It's becoming steeper and less uniform. More than any other single factor, terrain influences the way we ski.

Your instructor will spend some time talking about ways of "refining" your turns. The teacher will be particularly interested in the skidding phase.

By asking you to ski a lot, and demonstrating often, your instructor will encourage you to "back the skid up through the turn"—letting the skid appear earlier and earlier. In a very basic christy, for instance, you execute a wedge turn, wait until you're well past the fall line, and *then* add on a short skid.

As you work your way toward an intermediate christy, the skid will happen sooner and sooner, until your skis are being matched just after you cross the fall line.

4A.1

4A.2

4A.3

4A.4

4A.5

4A.6

Together you will work on refining the skid in other ways. You may spend some time examining your own tracks. They are your personal signature in the snow, and they tell you a lot about what's going on.

The skidding of the skis should be rounder and more fluid. At first your tracks will have sharp corners, like Zs. Later your tracks should look more like elongated Ss.

At first your skid tracks will be very wide. That's because your skid (sliding plus slipping, remember) will have more slip than slide. Later your tracks will get narrower as your skid has a higher percentage of forward sliding, and less sideslipping.

EXTENSION, FLEXION AND EDGE CONTROL

The instructor will also talk about *extension* (making yourself longer by coming "up") and *flexion* (going "down" to make your stance shorter).

By moving your center of mass, which we earlier nicknamed the "bowling ball," further from the snow or closer to the snow, you can increase pressure or ease pressure on your skis.

Flexing and extending are also closely tied in with *edge control,* something you have been learning all along. Generally, when we extend to come up very tall (as in the traverse side-slip) our edges are released and the skis flatten.

When the edges are released, pressure is usually released as well. This is a good time to turn the skis, because without edge or pressure, they pivot easily.

As we turn, we involve the foot, the whole leg and then the knee. The ski is edged more and more.

The more we turn (and edge) the more we flex our legs. The whole idea of flexion is to tip our shin bone against the side of the boot so we can lever the ski toward its edge.

"Down" motion, then, usually means stronger turning, more edging and added pressure.

Basically, "up" releases pressure—"down" adds pressure. Later, when we are skiing much faster, we will amend this last statement.

CENTRIFUGAL AND CENTRIPETAL FORCES

We have already mentioned centrifugal force. It's an important factor that acts on us while we are skiing. It's easiest to understand in this way:

If you attach a string to a tennis ball and swing the ball around your head, the ball travels in a circle. What we should notice most is that as long as the ball is in motion, the string stays tight.

Centrifugal force constantly pulls the ball away from our hand, which is at the center of the circle. Whenever a body (like a skier) travels in a curved path (through a skiing turn) centrifugal force keeps trying to pull us to the outside of the turn. You have already felt this.

If the string breaks, the ball would fly off in a straight line. The string, which keeps the ball in its curved path, represents *centripetal force.* Centripetal force keeps a body moving in a curved arc. It creates and holds us in the turn.

In the case of a skier, we have no string to keep us on a curved path. The only thing that keeps us from flying out of the turn is the friction we create with our edges.

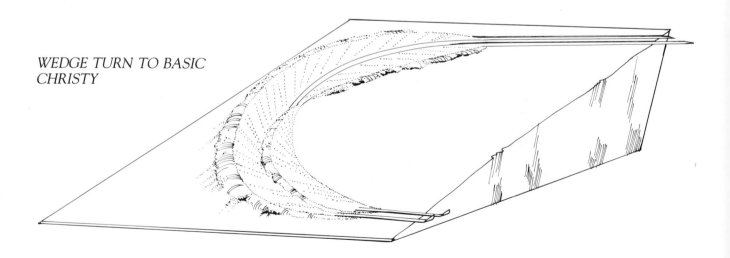

WEDGE TURN TO BASIC CHRISTY

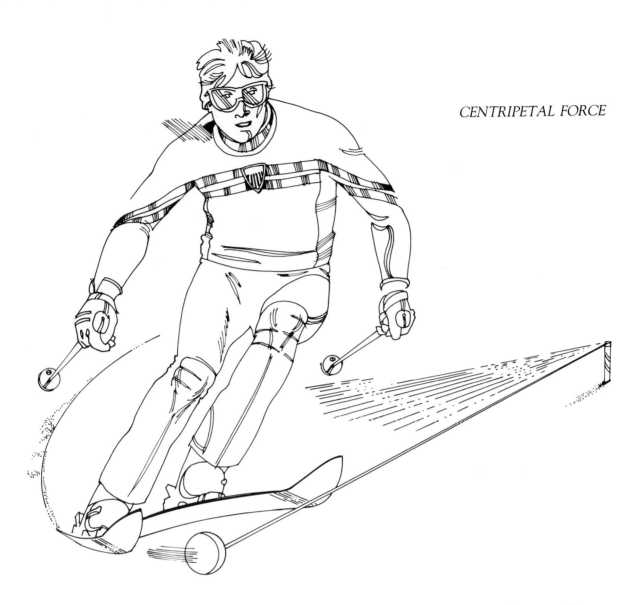

Centrifugal force is external. It's always acting upon us whenever we turn. To counteract it, we must resist internally, actively using our muscles to build centripetal force. We create centripetal force—in the form of friction—to help us deal with centrifugal force.

Centrifugal force helps us skid. Centripetal force helps control the skid, making our turns round.

Your body knows all this already. And some physicists might have a problem with such an oversimplified explanation. But the point to remember is that centrifugal force, gravity, friction, and centripetal force are all physical facts of skiing.

It helps to know about them, and understand the affects, but we needn't dwell on them to ski well.

Skidding

Most turns from here on out will be skidded. A skid that's just right for any given turn calls for delicate management of the ski on the snow. This means *edge control.* All three skiing skills—turning, edging and pressure control—must blend together.

At the beginning of the turns you are making now, say "Hi!" to yourself. The greeting is a reminder to come up into a small wedge, as follows.

Say "Hi!" once your edges are released. Then turn toward the fall line.

Match your skis when you have passed the fall line. Your skis will start to skid. To control the skid you should stay balanced on the middle of your skis. Gradually settle lower as you edge more and more. When your tips point toward the new traverse, come down still more, pushing your knees into the hill.

Sink to give extra edge to stop the skid. Now you're in a traverse. Again, if your mind refuses to absorb all this at once, that's OK. Your mind doesn't *have* to learn it. Your feet and legs do. We learn to ski by skiing, not by talking about it.

Class C: Intermediate Christies **71**

POLE-PLANT

We have used our poles to help us walk, and to help us sidestep, but up to this point, while moving at least, our poles have been little more than window dressing. Let's put them to use.

The pole has several functions. It's a steadying device. It steadies us when we walk, it holds us, and it helps us propel ourselves. It also steadies us when we ski. Keep in mind, though, that it's mostly a feeler that lets us know where the snow is. It's never a crutch to lean on.

The pole is also a timing device. It signals us when to come up, when to go down, and when to match. The bottom line is that the pole is an extension of our fingers which allows us to reach the ground with our hands.

When we ski and touch the tip of the pole to the snow, we make what's called a *pole-plant*. A pole-plant is never a harsh jab. It's a gentle placement of the pole tip in the snow.

From your very first straight run, you've been told to hold your hands up, forward and where you can see them. Your instructor may have been asking, "Are your hands ready?" There is a method to this madness.

If you are in the habit of keeping arms relaxed and hands within your field of vision, you are always ready to plant your pole. [4B.1]

There is no need to change the position of your hands as you plant the pole. Simply swing the tip of the pole forward with your wrist, and tap the snow with it. [4B.2]

There is sometimes confusion about which pole to plant as we turn. Always plant your right pole for right turns; your left pole for left turns. In a sense you are going to turn *around* the pole.

When you are traversing, get ready to swing your downhill pole. Swing it forward with your wrist.

If the fall line is to your right, you will make a right turn. If the fall line is to your left, you are going to make a left turn. Some intermediate skiers have success by thinking of their pole as a directional signal.

Recite those two musts over and over to yourself. Brand them into your mind. Not having to think about which pole to plant will help you later.

Make your very first pole-plants while you are in the fall line.

4B.1
KEEP YOUR HANDS READY

4B.2
PLANT THE POLE WITH WRIST AND FOREARM ACTION

Pole-Plant Timing

Do a straight wedge, right down the hill. Make sure your hands are ready. [4C.1]

Get set to turn out of the fall line, so your skis will point to the left. Weight your right ski—the one that's pointing left, where you want to go. Ready your left pole. [4C.2]

Swing it forward with your left wrist, and touch the snow with the tip. [4C.3]

Your pole-plant briefly gives you a third point of contact with the snow—two feet plus one pole. Take this golden opportunity to lift your light, inside ski and match it to your heavy, outside ski. [4C.4]

The match will inspire a skid. You might actually christy to a stop. [4C.5]

At this point in your skiing career, the pole-plant signals match! The pole steadies you as you do so.

Do the same maneuver, turning the other way.

4C.1
WEDGE

4C.2
READY

4C.3
TOUCH

4C.4
MATCH

4C.5
SKID

Planting The Correct Pole

Before you make a full turn, from one traverse to another, make *sure* there's no confusion about which pole you are going to plant.

Stand still, as though you were traversing. [4D.1]

Open to a wedge. [4D.2]

Notice the the fall line is to your left. To get to it, you must make a left turn. "Left pole for left turns." Swing your left pole forward, as though you were about to plant it, and hold it ready. Don't touch the snow yet. [4D.3]

Though it seems repetitious and ridiculous, do the same thing while you're moving in a traverse. Traverse . . . wedge . . . ready your downhill pole.

Ski all the way across the slope, grooving this feeling into your muscle memory. Traverse . . . wedge . . . poise the downhill pole. Close your skis . . . traverse . . . wedge . . . poise the downhill pole.

Traverse back to the opposite edge of the slope. Obviously you will now be readying your other pole.

4D.1
TRAVERSE

4D.2
WEDGE

4D.3
POISE THE POLE

THINKING ON THE INTERMEDIATE CHRISTY

The *intermediate christy* is sometimes called a "wedge christy with a pole-plant." It's the culmination of Class C.

It may be helpful to divide the turn into three parts:

1) the *top* where the turn is initiated,

2) the fall line phase at the *middle* of the turn, and

3) the *bottom,* where the turn is completed.

Let's take it from the top. Any intermediate christy begins with a traverse, an opening of the skis to a wedge, and a readying of the correct pole. You have already practiced these.

The pole-plant and the match are done when you face right down the fall line. Then a lot happens all at once—at a time when we feel gravity most intensely. That's when the pole becomes truly helpful. It steadies us at this critical time.

Once the skis are matched, we're into the bottom of the turn—the completion phase. Here we are skidding. The skid should be smooth, fairly narrow, and round. We end the skid whenever we start traversing again.

Putting an intermediate christy together should be simple. You have all the parts in your muscle-memory bank already. It's just a matter of putting them together.

As with any skiing turn you're about to try for the very first time, it helps to see it through in your mind's eye beforehand—imagining each step. This sort of mental preview is called *pre-visualization*.

Your instructor will have demonstrated the maneuver beforehand. Imagine yourself doing just what you saw.

4E.1
NATURAL STANCE

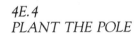

4E.2
WEDGE

4E.3
TURN AND POISE THE POLE

4E.4
PLANT THE POLE

4E.5
MATCH

MILESTONE #6: INTERMEDIATE CHRISTY

Here we go. Good traverse. Balanced in the middle of the skis. All joints flexed. Hands ready. [4E.1]

Come up, spreading your tails into a wedge. The wedge doesn't have to be very wide. [4E.2]

Ready the inside pole with your wrist as you start steering to the fall line. Hold the pole with the tip just forward of vertical. Transfer weight to the outside ski, so pressure is lessened on the inside ski. [4E.3]

When you face the fall line you will feel acceleration. Plant the inside pole now. [4E.4]

Use the brief stability of the pole-plant to help you match the light ski to the heavy outside ski. [4E.5]

Skid both skis. Control the skid by gradually settling lower, flexing your legs to coax the skis onto a higher and higher edge. [4E.6]

The skid, and the intermediate christy itself, ends when the traverse begins. [4E.7]

Make lots of these intermediate christies. Take long runs, linking them together.

4E.6
SKID

4E.7
TRAVERSE

WHAT YOU SHOULD FEEL

At this stage you probably feel like a robot. Composing a new turn is like painting by the numbers. We paint in the right spaces, but the colors don't flow together yet.

Of all the art forms, skiing most resembles dance. Dancers take classes to be trained in individual movements. Later these moves are combined as the dancer expresses himself.

Start to dance.

Ski classes are meant to help you learn *technique*—a sequence of movements that get the job done. Technique is what works, so there are dozens of techniques. You already know many.

Earlier we mentioned *style*—the way each of us "dances" on skis. Our own unique style is born out of the very personal way we put various techniques together.

Start to be aware of your own skiing style. But remember that style must have its basis in sound technique.

We develop style through experimentation and *mileage*. The only way to put things together is to ski lots and lots of miles. There is no substitute for mileage.

As you prepare for Class D, concentrate on these things:

♦ Let your movements flow together. No step in the intermediate christy, for example, should be isolated from the next.

♦ Let the down movement that ends your first turn become a lifting into the next. By feeling this, see if you can make your traverses disappear altogether.

♦ Reduce the size of your wedges whenever it feels comfortable.

♦ Match your skis at the fall line, then *before* the fall line, if you can.

♦ Use the pole as dancers use their hands. It's a wand, an antenna, a feeler. It will help you with balance, rhythm, and timing. Be disciplined with your pole. Keep your pole movements simple. Hold your hands where you can see them and swing the pole tip forward with your wrist. Develop a light touch.

Getting Tired

In skiing we tend to tire *before* we realize it. When you start to fall, when you seem to make a lot of mistakes, when techniques you already know don't work any longer, fatigue is creeping in.

Quit for the day.

Advanced Wedge Christies

We're fast approaching the turn that every new skier dreams of making—a parallel turn. In fact, we're so close, you can probably taste it. Hold your horses. Don't rush the parallel turn. And don't skip Class D!

At this stage too many intermediates say to themselves, "I want to ski parallel. I'm going to put my feet together and make everything work."

That's the wrong approach. Do that and you will start to make some gross errors that can easily become bad habits—habits you may never break.

Better to say, "If I make everything work, my feet will come together."

As you study technique, or watch another skier's style, start at the snow and let your eyes work up. The temptation will be to do just the opposite: to watch another's upper body (which is larger and more obvious) and then work down.

Remember that skiing really happens between the bottoms of the skis and the snow. Every move you make should enhance the snow-ski contact that's happening.

If everything is right at snow level, chances are that everything will look right in the rest of the body. Ski from the snow up!

CHRISTIES

A christy, as we've already said, is any turn that involves a skid. Skidding, is a combination of sliding and slipping, if you remember. To skid in a christy we need some speed, but we don't need to have our skis parallel to make a christy.

Stem Christy (Pointing Christy)

The term *stem* comes to us from German. You might think of a stem as half a wedge. We often "stem" as we traverse, and as we begin turns. When we ski across the hill we open to a half-wedge and point our uphill ski toward the fall line.

If we follow a stem with a turn, we make what German-speaking skiers would call a *stem christy*. American instructors may call it a *pointing christy*. They are practically the same turn.

Pointing (or stemming) at first has little or nothing to do with the downhill ski. We are primarily concerned with what the uphill ski is doing.

As we point the uphill ski toward the fall line, the downhill ski can either hold its edge, or break loose and wedge slightly as well. We call this a *double stem*. Either action is acceptable.

At this stage, stemming helps in several ways. First, it stabilizes us as we enter the fall line because by widening our feet, we give ourselves a broader base of support.

Second, because the stem puts us on our two inside edges, it gives us a chance to slow down, if we need to, as we enter the fall line. In that way the stem is like the wedge. Even super-expert skiers use pointing christies in very difficult or dangerous snow conditions.

Third, as we stem, a turn is already half started for us. Fourth, by stemming we automatically make an *edge-change* with one ski—before the turn begins.

Every time we ski from one turn to another we have to cross the fall line. Crossing the fall line always requires an edge-change. We change-edges by rolling the ski past flat to it's opposite edge.

In a pointing christy we first change the edge of one ski by stemming . . . then we change the edge of the other. It's a one-two edge-change.

A parallel christy differs from an advanced pointing christy in just one fundamental way: when we make a parallel turn, we change both edges of both skis at the same time. Otherwise, pointing christies and parallel christies are all but identical.

Learning to make excellent pointing christies is worth the effort.

Pointing Christies Without Pole-Plant

After you have practiced traversing and pointing your uphill ski into a stem, try a pointing christy without a pole-plant. It looks like this:

Ski in a fairly steep traverse—closer to the fall line—rather than a very flat traverse that requires you to turn farther. A steeper traverse also gives you more speed to work with. Stand tall. [5A.1]

Open to a half-wedge by pointing your uphill ski toward the fall line. Brush the tail of the uphill ski away from the downhill ski. This is "stemming." If the edge of the downhill ski breaks loose while you stem, that's OK. Notice how the uphill ski is pointing more than the downhill ski is holding. [5A.2]

Weight both skis and steer toward the fall line. Gradually transfer more weight to the outside ski—the one you pointed at the fall line in the first place. [5A.3]

Now brush the tail of the lightened inside ski toward the tail of the outside ski. This is matching. [5A.4]

Once you have matched, complete the turn with a skid. During the skid you will gradually edge more and allow pressure to build on the skis. This lowers your stance at the end of the turn. You may want to rise up as you begin the next traverse. [5A.5]

A pointing christy without a pole-plant might feel suspiciously like the intermediate christy you already know. It is. The difference comes at the beginning of the turn where you point one or both skis.

At this time you should be starting to develop an awareness of edge-change. When you traverse, notice that both skis are on their uphill edges. It's possible to stem out with your uphill ski without losing the edge of your downhill ski at all.

Practice that too. It will help you when the snow is very slippery.

Once you point the uphill ski, you are on opposing edges—just as you are in a wedge. That is, by stemming you have changed the edge of your uphill ski. [See 5A.2 again]

Later in the turn, when you match, you also change the edge of the second ski. [5A.4 again] The edges of both skis have been changed, but at different times.

Let's take this a step further.

5A.1
TRAVERSE

5A.2
POINT

5A.3
TURN

5A.4
MATCH

5A.5
EDGE AND PRESS

Class D: Advanced Wedge Christies **79**

Pointing Christies
With Pole-Plant

As your technique gets more sophisticated, the pole plays a larger and larger role in your skiing. At first it tells you when to match the skis. Later it triggers up motion and the edge-change itself.

Pole-plant timing becomes critical in a pointing (stem) christy.

More advanced turns end with edging and pressure build-up. The result is a flexing in the legs—down motion.

We already know that when we link turns together, and eliminate the traverse, the down motion that "sets" the edges at the end the first turn must turn into up motion to "release" the edges for the next.

As we get better, we don't have time to rise up for the traverse, because there *is* no traverse. Approach your first pointing christies with a pole-plant in a lower stance, pretending there's no traverse. Make sure your hands are in a ready position. [5B.1]

Rise and stem with one or both skis. That's edge-change number one. As you stem, swing the tip of the pole forward with your wrist. Remember, right pole for right turns; left pole for left turns. [5B.2]

Touch the pole to the snow. That's your signal to match, which becomes the second edge-change. [5B.3]

Be light with your pole-plant. There's no need to lean on it. The match, remember, will stimulate a skid. [5B.4]

Round out the skid by adding edge and pressure. As always, edging more makes your knees bend more, causing your center of mass to go "down." Are you in a ready stance for the next turn?

5B.2
RISE AND READY THE POLE

5B.3
PLANT AND MATCH

5B.4
SKID

5B.1
STAND LOW

5B.5
EDGE, PRESS AND SINK

The answer should be, "yes." [5B.5]

The sinking to finish this turn offers a chance to rise into the next. Rhythm should now come into play. Make your stems smaller. Ready your pole earlier.

Instead of planting and matching just before the fall line [as in 5B.3], match your skis well *before* the fall line. Instead of rising, readying the pole, then planting and matching, try to let the pole-plant trigger a simultaneous up-and-matching movement.

If the pole-plant tells you to come up and match early, and you do that, you will have changed both edges of both skis before the fall line. The rest of the turn will be made with your skis more or less parallel.

You're already 75% through a parallel turn.

Now ski lots of miles, making pointing christies with pole-plants.

WHAT TO AVOID

Now is the time to avoid pitfalls that could plague you later on.

Always keep your upper body facing where you're going—or where you're about to go. It's OK to "anticipate" a turn that's coming up, by turning your upper body toward the turn a little early. This anticipation will become very helpful later on. [5C]

To be sure your torso faces the way you're going (or are about to go), *look* where you're going—just as you were taught in your very first straight run. Are both hands ready, and can you see both hands? [5C again]

Over-Rotation

If you come through a turn and discover you have lost sight of your inside hand, you have rotated your upper body much faster than than your skis have turned. You're now facing uphill, away from the next turn. That's a no-no called *over-rotating*. [5D]

Under-Rotation

If you end a turn and you lose sight of your outside hand, you have turned your upper body much slower than the skis. As you'd expect, this is called *under-rotating*. [5E]

Under-rotating is not as serious as over-rotating. At least you're facing downhill—toward the new turn. But it can lead to worse problems later.

Hip Rotation

Are you afraid you can't make three-quarters of the turn with your skis parallel? If so, you may try to give yourself more turning power by rotating your hips. *Hip rotation* is another serious no-no.

5C
ANTICIPATE

We have tremendous turning power in our hips. (That's why golfers rotate their hips when they drive.) The trouble is we have *too* much power there—power we can't control.

What's even worse is that strong power source is too far removed from the snow.

Don't forget, we must ski from the snow up. To do so (and to ski properly), we must turn primarily with our feet, knees and legs—parts closest to the snow.

We have to cool it with our hips. If we don't, we apply too much raw torque to the skis. *Overturning* is the result. When we overturn, our tips climb back up the hill too far, and we're completely out of position for the next turn (5D again).

Keep your hips "quiet." Like your upper body, let them turn at about the same speed your skis are turning [Check sequence 5B again] to guarantee that your hips don't rotate.

The point to recall is that rotation problems—under-rotation and over-rotation, which includes hip rotation—are caused by a lack of proper turning power in the lower body. Ironically, rotation can cause overturning.

A large part of your time in Class D may be spent heading off the problems of over-rotation, under-rotation, hip rotation and overturning. These errors can creep back into our skiing at any time from here on out.

5D
TRY NOT TO OVER-ROTATE

FLUID MOVEMENT

This is an intangible but crucial factor. A *very* good skier has technique peculiarities that distinguish him or her from the pretty good skier. That extra ingredient is coordinated *fluid movement*.

To ski well, we must always be moving—not only over the snow, but bodily. All movements should be connected. No part of us should ever be static. Sometimes the movements are quick, sometimes they are more drawn-out. But you should always be in motion.

In most terrain situations, we constantly turn. Traverses will appear only when we get off balance and need to get our act together again.

If we are always making curved tracks in the snow, we are either finishing, beginning, or in the midst of a turn. We are forever in the process of either making ourselves taller or shorter, moving our center of mass closer to, or away from the snow surface.

Our legs are either flexing or extending, our knees are bending or straightening, and our hands are always moving within their own limited sphere of readiness—often moving ahead for the next pole-plant. That's fluid movement.

Fluid movement should become evident in your skiing by the end of Class D.

5E
TRY NOT TO
UNDER-ROTATE

Class D: Advanced Wedge Christies **83**

MILESTONE #7: ADVANCED POINTING CHRISTIES

To show fluid movement you can't think of turns as isolated sequences of positions. Always be aware of how each turn relates to the one before it, and the one that will come after.

You will approach an advanced pointing christy quite low because you will have flexed to edge and built pressure at the end of the previous turn. Your belly button points where you are going and both hands are in sight. The downhill wrist is ready. [5F.1]

Weight is on the downhill ski. The pole swings forward and the skis are stemmed. By opening the feet you will sink lower still. You're like a cat ready to spring into action. [5F.2]

Use the pole-plant to trigger up motion. Rise up and forward as you match. Both edges have now been changed. [5F.3]

The match automatically transfers weight to your outside ski—the ski that's about to become your downhill ski. Now, without twisting your upper body or hips, turn your feet and legs—exactly as you did in wedge turns. This controls the skid. [5F.4]

Once past the fall line, refine the skid by adding edge and pressure. As soon as you have turned far enough out of the fall line to control your speed, you should be ready to begin your next turn. [5F.5]

The most critical point in the advanced pointing christy happens as you plant and come up (See 5F.3 once more). The up movement makes you feel momentarily "light," and makes the rest of the turn easy. At the "up," you are also making that second important edge-change.

Don't loose your balance as you come up. The pole is there to steady you.

Let all of your movements work in harmony with each other. Practice making big, round pointing christies. Each movement will last longer in these extended turns. You'll feel as though you're working in slow motion. Nonetheless, everything still moves continuously.

Practice making shorter pointing christies. Everything must now happen faster as you make tighter turns. You'll feel like you're running on "fast-forward." Most normal turns are somewhere between these two extremes—long-radius turns and short-radius turns.

Which are easier for you, short radius turns, or long radius turns? (Surprising answer: shorter turns.) Can you guess why?

Reason: Shorter movements, which last less time, are easier to control than long, drawn-out motions.

Make your stems smaller and smaller. Stem earlier and earlier. Put some "umph" into your up motion. Change both edges earlier and earlier.

Ski lots. Maybe, before you know it, the stem will disappear altogether, and you'll be skiing parallel.

5F.1
READY

5F.5
EDGE AND PRESS

5F.2
POINT

5F.3
POLE-PLANT—UP MOTION!

5F.4
TURN

CLASS E

Parallel Turns

At this stage, you'll have plenty of company. Aside from the beginner's class, Class E is far and away the most popular lesson in the ATM progression. Everybody wants to "ski with their feet together." People who have never taken a ski lesson in their lives will show up for this one.

During the ski-off, the split supervisor must separate those struggling with bad habits from those who have learned to make a reasonable pointing christy. Sometimes new students who show up for "E" end up being assigned to "D" for background and extra help.

If you have stayed with the program so far—without skipping anything—you should look like a pro. Your class may be a mixture of ski-school regulars like yourself (some of whom have taken "E" before) and newcomers.

The transition from pointing turns to parallel turns *is* a big one. In fact, some skiers can never get there, especially those who have gotten too good at making a standard stem christy.

In years past a parallel skier was the exception rather than the rule. Today, with modern equipment, good instruction and well-groomed ski runs, almost anybody can ski parallel in just a few days. Now, on intermediate slopes everywhere, at least 90% of the skiers you see make some semblance of a parallel turn.

But that's not to say they're all skiing correctly.

WHAT PARALLEL MEANS

As we know, parallel lines never cross. No matter how far they extend, they remain the same distance apart at all points—forever.

In skiing, our definition of parallel is not so strict. Basically we mean that both skis point in more or less the same direction, as they do when we make a straight run or a traverse. That means you have already done some parallel skiing.

When we make a parallel turn, both feet, both legs, and both knees work at the same time. Instructors, including us, use the term *simultaneous leg rotation* to describe what happens, even though technically, it's impossible to rotate both legs at precisely the same instant.

The difference between the pointing christy, learned at the D level, and a parallel christy learned in E, centers on edge change.

When we point (or stem), we change edges one at a time, by turning one leg, then the other, then both. We call this *independent leg rotation*.

As we mentioned in the last chapter, the unique ingredient in the parallel turn is *simultaneous edge change*. Both edges of both skis are changed at the same time. *Simultaneous edge change is really what any parallel turn is all about.*

To change edges simultaneously, and to rotate both lower limbs at the same time, it helps to open our feet up. With our feet apart, we can not only move more effectively, we also stay out of our own way. For instance, our knees don't bump into each other.

In fact, many intermediates who are learning to make parallel turns find it very helpful to open their feet beyond an "open stance." We call this *wide track.*

Wide track has several benefits. First it's more stable than a narrow, "closed" stance. Second, it's easy to go from a wide track to a wedge or a stem if we need to.

Third, it lets us edge either ski very easily. Fourth, and most important, it allows us to feel immediate results when we transfer weight from one foot to the other.

what you want to accomplish on the snow. Racers and other "experts" understand that if you can do it better, or get there faster, by letting your feet operate separately, then that's what you should do.

Parallel skiing is not something to get hung up on. Many skiers are so concerned about making two skis act like one, that they go into incredible contortions with their legs, arms, hips and upper bodies in an effort to imitate what they think very good skiers do.

Keeping your feet and knees clutched together at all costs puts you in a "locked" stance. Parallel does not mean lower body restriction.

WHAT PARALLEL DOES NOT MEAN

You are never going to believe it until after you've mastered the parallel turn, but the parallel *is not* the ultimate goal of ski technique. Beginners and the very best skiers in the world have one thing in common: they have their skies parallel only some of the time.

Trying to ski parallel must never interfere with

Right And Wrong

To get enough edge on the downhill ski, the "clutcher" tucks one knee in behind the other. That works OK for a single traverse, but to turn you have to untuck one knee, change your lead ski, and then retuck the other knee when you're going the other way. It's too complicated, awkward and uncomfortable. [6A]

What clutchers focus on is the fact that during the middle of a parallel turn better skiers have their feet tight together. Centrifugal force makes that happen.

What clutchers *don't* see is that before parallel turns, and after parallel turns, very good skiers open their feet so their legs can work freely and efficiently. Like this: [6B]

Let's get on with making parallel turns.

6A
DON'T CLUTCH YOUR KNEES TOGETHER

6B
OPEN YOUR STANCE

WHERE YOU ARE NOW

During the ski off at the beginning of Class E, you should be making a turn about like this one.

You approach your best turn in a low and ready stance, as though you have just completed a previous turn. [6C.1]

As you swing the pole tip forward to plant the pole, you rise and separate your feet, widening your stance. You might stem to turn the uphill ski toward the fall line. That's OK. A stem should *never* be thought of as "bad". [6C.1]

Plant and match your skis as you begin to skid. The combination of your match, plus centrifugal force, pulls your feet together. Both skis drift out from under your body, seeking an edge. [6C.2]

Turn the skis as they slip out to the side. Once they're out from under you far enough, they will be on edge. Turn your legs to increase the edge. [6C.3]

Flex your knees forward and into the hill to increase edging and pressure on the skis. This will lower your stance again as you complete the turn. [6C.4]

You already know all that. Now it's time to convince yourself that you can make a turn without stemming at all.

6C.1
STAND LOW

6C.2
OPEN AND STAND TALLER

6C.3
PLANT-UP AND MATCH

6C.4
EDGE

6C.5
PRESS

Patience Turns

These should be done on a wide and gentle slope. Don't try them on terrain that intimidates you in any way. It will take the skis some time to reach the fall line. As the name suggests, you have to be patient.

Start in a low traverse with most of your weight on the downhill ski. To hold, your knees will have to be pushed into the hill somewhat. Make sure your stance is open enough to allow both knees freedom to edge the skis comfortably. [6D.1]

As usual, the way to release your edges is to rise up. This moves your knees away from the hill and flattens the skis. The releasing sensation will be just like the feeling of the traverse sideslip you learned in Class C. [6D.2]

Gently press forward against your boot tongue as the skis slip. Begin to weight both skis, stay balanced, steer ever so slightly, and be patient. The ski tips will gradually turn downhill—toward the fall line. As they point downhill, ready the pole for a plant. [6D.3]

Plant the inside pole and pivot your feet. Because the skis are so flat, they will be very easy to turn. [6D.4]

Edge with your legs while you are turning. Centrifugal force brings your feet closer together. Let them come together. [6D.5]

Transfer more weight to the new downhill ski as you come out of the fall line. [6D.6]

Flex the knees forward, edging more and adding pressure to the downhill ski. [6D.7]

You have just made your first parallel turn. Nothing to it, right?

You have also had an object lesson in what happens when friction at your edges is removed by rising up. With a little downhill steering and nothing to keep your skis from moving across the slope, eventually they will find the fall line.

The patience turn is fine, as long as you have plenty of time and plenty of room to let the turn develop. Unfortunately we don't always have that much time and space. Happily there are ways to hasten this very slow entry into the fall line.

6D.1
STAND LOW TO HOLD

6D.7
PRESS

6D.2
UP TO RELEASE

6D.3
LET THE SKIS FIND THE
FALL LINE

6D.4
PLANT AND PIVOT

6D.5
EDGE

6D.6
SHIFT WEIGHT

UNWEIGHTING

This is a word we use to describe various ways of taking pressure off our skis for a very short period of time. By making ourselves "lighter," even for a split second, we can release our edges and pivot both skis downhill faster and more easily.

Unweighting is not necessary in every turn, but it's a big help to any intermediate learning to make parallel turns. It's also part of any expert's repertoire. Very good skiers unweight in heavy, wet snow, and even on ice. It should be part of *your* bag of tricks, too.

There are four methods of getting lighter. Two ways of unweighting—up and down—are "internal." That is, unweighting that involves the use of our own muscles.

Another method is "external." In this case we allow something outside our bodies to act upon us. In the fourth case, a combination of external and internal forces unweights us.

The most important thing to remember about unweighting is that the lightness we experience is very brief. We must take advantage of it right away or we'll lose it. Obviously timing and balance are important.

Up Unweighting

Stand on your bathroom scale at home, crouching low. Then quickly lift your center of mass (without jumping). You will make the needle on the scale bounce downward by 70 or 80 pounds—it then bounces right back up.

It is like throwing a bowling ball into the air. The ball travels up, hesitate at its highest point, and then comes back down.

At the highest point of the up, during that split second when the ball hesitates before reversing direction, it is relatively weightless. If the "bowling ball" is your center of mass, you are said to be *unweighted* at that point.

The beauty of up unweighting, relative to other forms of unweighting, is that although the "light" period is very brief, it lasts a fairly long time compared to down unweighting. That's why we concentrate on up unweighting first.

When we're skiing, we have to recognize a couple of things about up unweighting. First of all, we're in motion when we're on skis. That makes tossing the bowling ball straight up tricky.

We have to realize we're on a slope and that our skis are pointing down this inclined plane. The slope is what keeps us moving.

Down Unweighting

This is somewhat harder to accomplish, although you will surely learn how to down unweight as you become an expert skier.

Starid on the bathroom scale at home again. Extend your legs so you are standing quite tall. Then suddenly drop your center of mass by bending your knees. You just down unweighted. The lightness happens the instant the bowling ball starts to drop. In other words, the lightness doesn't last as long as with down-*up*-down.

The other difference—and difficulty—is that when you down unweight you must sink and turn all at once. You don't have extension, unweighting, then flexion to turn. You have to drop and apply torque all in one movement.

Don't get us wrong. Down unweighting has its advantages, especially on very hard, slippery snow—when you *don't* want to be light and have your edges released for a very long time.

A few skiers down unweight naturally, without ever being taught. They will do so from the very beginning and might actually find up unweighting quite difficult. If that's the case with you, it's OK but later your challenge will be to learn other easier forms of unweighting.

Terrain Unweighting

We have all been launched, at one time or another, by a small bump or ripple in the snow. We'll be skiing along and then some irregularity in the terrain gives us an unexpected lift. *Expect* rises in the terrain to do that to you. You can use it to your advantage.

The bump is, in effect, tossing your bowling ball up. When you get to the top of the up movement caused by the terrain, you are up unweighted. Use this lightness and turn right away.

You can stay down as long as you like. But the lightness at the top of the up happens very quickly. Once you're up, you must come down immediately, applying some turning force. If you stay up, the lightness disappears, and you might as well have not unweighted at all.

You already know that when you turn your legs and flex your knees, you are exerting rotary forces on the skis. In this case down motion *is* turning force.

This means we must have direction in our up movement, coming up and *toward* the new turn as we unweight so we don't lose our balance backwards and let the skis accelerate out from under us.

Second, when you hear ski instructors coaching their students in unweighting, they often say, "Down . . . up . . . down." Actually the movement should be more like "down . . . updown." Can you hear the difference?

Good instructors may use a specific piece of terrain to help skiers make their very first parallel turns. They will find a gentle bump that can unweight a student without a loss of balance. The student skis up on the bump, gets a lift, and feels how easy it is to turn both skis at the same time.

Recognize that irregular terrain is not necessarily a mine field fraught with all kinds of pitfalls and hazards. Bumps can actually be helpful, and will become more so as you improve.

Rebound Unweighting

It's also possible to, in effect, "bounce" your bowling ball off the snow. Our center of mass doesn't actually hit the ground because our legs are there to support us, but we can unweight with the help of "rebound" from both our skis and our muscles.

Have you ridden a descending elevator that suddenly stopped? It felt as though the floor of the elevator was pushing upward. Your knees gave a little bit, and then you sprung back to your normal height with a slight jerk.

Your muscles were compressed by extra G forces, the total force you feel from gravity and deceleration caused by the elevator's abrupt stop. Your joints flexed in reaction. By reflex, your muscles then stretched back to their normal length and you were upright again. In short, when we're squashed down, we want to pop right back up.

The same thing happens while we are skiing. Gravity is pulling us downhill. We suddenly create a lot of friction and stop (or slow) our downhill progress by edging and turning our skis. The skis suddenly bend into reverse camber, losing their natural arch. (See page 49.)

After the edges set, the skis snap back to their original shape, and the compressed muscles in our legs stretch back to their normal length. The combination causes the bowling ball to "rebound" away from the snow. We are again momentarily light. Turning is easy right after any rebound.

Rebound occurs most often as we are making short parallel turns in succession. We call this *shortswing*. It will be covered in the next chapter.

FOOLPROOF FAN

The fan approach teaches just about anybody to ski parallel. The term *fan* describes not the action, but the tracks you will have made in the snow after a series of parallel maneuvers.

In the fan, we sneak up on the parallel turn by approaching it backward. We deal with the end phase of the turn, which you already know by now, and work toward the unweighting phase at the start of the turn.

First, we will ski across the slope and stop by making a parallel turn uphill—track #1. This is called an *uphill christy*.

Second, we will make another uphill christy, but from a steeper approach—track #2.

Third, we make an uphill christy to a stop, starting from the fall line. Then we do the same turn with a pole-plant—tracks #3 and #4. The pole-plant will help us with up unweighting.

Finally we will make a full turn across the fall line with a pole-plant and up unweighting—track #5.

6E.1
STAND HIGH

THE FOOLPROOF FAN

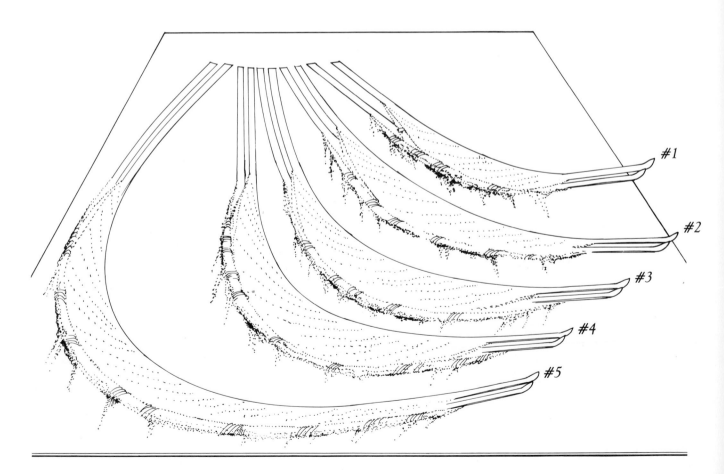

#1

#2

#3

#4

#5

6E.2
PUSH FORWARD AND TURN

6E.3
EDGE AND PRESS

Uphill Parallel Christy

In an uphill christy there is no need to cross the fall line, and therefore no need to transfer weight from one ski to another. You will keep your weight on the downhill ski for the entire time. There is also no need to unweight.

Start high, pretending that you have just up unweighted. Keep your feet separated enough to allow your legs plenty of freedom. The uphill ski, boot, knee, hip, hand and shoulder should lead. [6E.1]

As you gain some speed, press forward into your boots so the edges at the shovels of the ski engage. Steer with your legs as the ski tips begin to climb uphill. [6E.2]

Flex your knees forward to increase pressure on the edged ski, just as you have in all your recent turns. This will increase edge and increase pressure on your downhill ski. You will turn uphill to a stop. [6E.3]

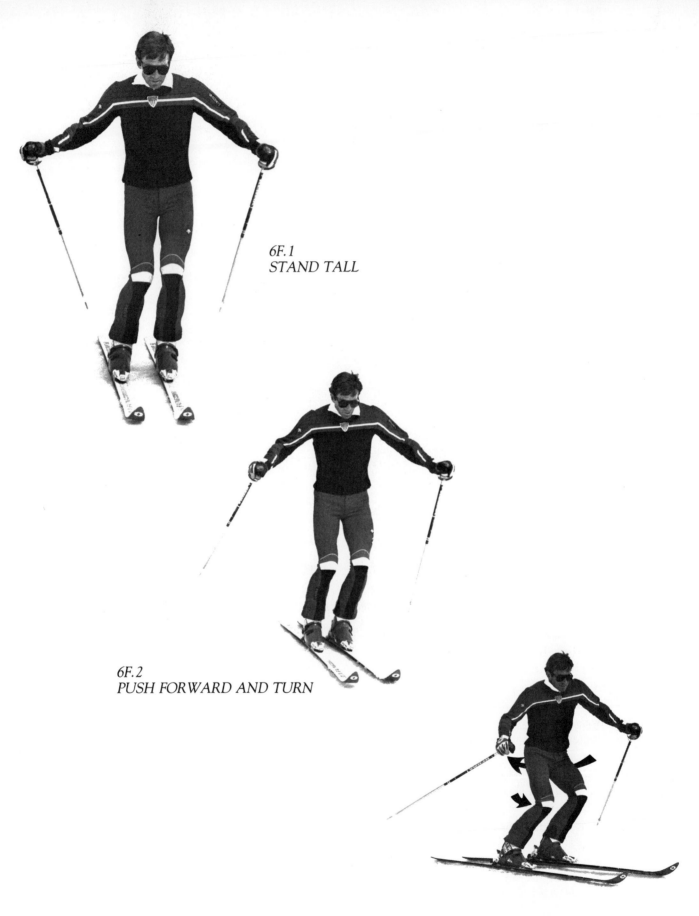

6F.1
STAND TALL

6F.2
PUSH FORWARD AND TURN

6F.3
COUNTER WITH THE HIP

Uphill Christy
From Steep Traverse

Next time point your skis more directly down the hill. You will have to turn farther this time, but the maneuver is basically the same.

Start high again, in an open stance. This is almost a straight run, so there will only be a slight lead with the side of your body closest to the turn—in this case the left side. [6F.1]

Gently push your shins into the tongues of your boots to exert some forward leverage on the skis. Turn both your legs at the same time. [6F.2]

As you flex your knees through the bottom of the uphill christy, allow your legs to turn faster than your upper body and hips. Your outside hip will be delayed. This holding back of the hip is called *countermovement*. [6F.3]

Edge and press to a stop. Notice how there is no clutching at the knees. Notice too how the uphill boot, knee, hip, hand and shoulder still lead, causing the whole body to face the valley.

Because the body is turned downhill it is "open"—receptive to the next turn. [6F.4]

"Old-time" ski instructors like us are fond of saying, "The hip controls the tail of the ski." In fact, it does.

If we hold the outside hip back, "countering" by making the hips turn slower than the skis, we accomplish three things:

♦ We put ourselves in a stronger position to withstand centrifugal force during the turn.

♦ We keep the tail of the ski from losing its edge and slipping out.

♦ We keep ourselves in a ready posture for the next turn.

As we explore the parallel turn further, you will begin to appreciate the value of countermovement more and more. But don't confuse countermovement (a holding back with the outside of the body) with *counterrotation* which we'll talk about in Class F.

6F.4
EDGE AND PRESS

6G.1
STAND HIGH

6G.2
TURN AND COUNTER

6G.3
EDGE AND PRESS

Uphill Christy From Fall Line

Remember that unweighting's purpose is to help get you to the fall line. We are still practicing the more difficult part of the turn—getting *out* of the fall line.

When your skis are pointing directly down the fall line, they will be right under you and and flat. This makes them very easy to turn. Don't worry about keeping them perfectly parallel, but try not to stem. [6G.1]

Pivot the skis while they're flat beneath you. Feel that your skis, feet, and legs are turning more rapidly than your shoulders. This will help you counter. [6G.2]

Edge as your legs turn, and flex your knees to push your shins into the fronts of the boots. This keeps the skis turning uphill. Stop, but feel that you are slightly countered as you come to a standstill. [6G.3]

6H.1
STAND LOW AND READY THE POLE

6H.2
PLANT

6H.3
UP AND PIVOT

6H.4
DOWN TO TURN AND EDGE

6H.5
PRESS

Uphill Christy From Fall Line With Pole-Plant

Now it's time to feel how the pole-plant aids in unweighting, and how unweighting aids turning.

Start in the fall line, but crouch a little lower this time. You can't come "up," if you aren't "down" to begin with. Ready your inside pole (left pole for left turns) and swing the pole tip forward. [6H.1]

Keep your stance open. Get the pole tip out in front of your feet so you will ski past it when it's planted. As the pole touches the snow, you will feel yourself pop up. [6H.2]

At the high point of the up, you will be light, and your skis will be very easy to turn because they have been so flat on the snow. Pivot your feet when you feel lightest. [6H.3]

Turning and edging will start to bring you back down again. Transfer weight to your outside (downhill) ski. As you skid your feet will come out from under you as the skis drift toward their edges. Feel countermovement. [6H.4]

Press your edges into the snow and come to a stop. [6H.5]

61.3
PLANT-UP

61.4
PIVOT

61.5
COUNTER AND EDGE

6I.1
STAND NEUTRAL

6I.2
DOWN AND READY TO
PLANT

Christy Across Fall Line With Pole-Plant

This is the moment of truth. Now we must make the last set of tracks in the fan, and make our first real parallel turn across the fall line.

Start in a normal traverse, standing neither high nor low. [6I.1]

Sink down and swing your downhill pole well forward—all in the same motion. [6I.2]

As you plant and ski past the pole, let that action force your center of mass upward. [6I.3]

Pivot your feet at the highest point of the up—when you are unweighted—and start your skid. You have made it to the fall line. This time, though, the unweighting and the skid have allowed your feet to move out from under you. [6I.4]

Now it's a question of finishing a turn as usual. Try to resist any urge to over-rotate and overturn. Stay countered as you shift weight to the downhill ski and edge. Your delayed hip will keep your tails from skidding out too fast. [6I.5]

Flex your knees, as always, through the remainder of the turn and stop. [6I.6]

You have just made a parallel turn, and done it right. Nice going!

6I.6
PRESS

MILESTONE #8:
PARALLEL CHRISTY
WITH POLE-PLANT

Once you move out of the fan drill, you begin to put the parallel turn into perspective. It's now a matter of skiing from one turn into another, passing through the fall line to get there.

You don't need to stop at the end of each turn, and you can begin to transfer your weight a little earlier. Starting a turn without a stem is like finally learning to ride a bike after hours of trying. Once you get it, you don't forget it.

Assist simultaneous leg rotation and simultaneous edge change by up unweighting. Feel fluid movement. Everything should start to flow.

Keep your feet separated. Prepare for each turn with a down motion, and a preparation of the pole. [6J.1]

Plant and rise up. Make sure you are coming up and into the turn so you don't let the skis slide out from under you. [6J.2]

Once you're up, you're light. Use the lightness right away. Turn your feet toward the fall line. You can begin to transfer weight now. [6J.3]

Your skis will skid out to the side toward their edges. [6J.4]

Once the skis have found their edges, steer them harder to keep them turning out of the fall line. Counter slightly. You should feel yourself lowering and pressing into the tip of your downhill ski. [6J.5]

Complete the turn with pressure and more down movement. [6J.6]

As you head toward the next turn, you should feel a small lead in the uphill skis, boot, knee, hip, hand and shoulder. This is a normal, comfortable, traversing stance. At this point you are "down" again. [6J.7]

Practice these turns. Make thousands of them. Don't try to remember all the details. Your turns will not be perfect at first. Try to "ski" each turn, concentrating on the initiation of each—the pole-plant and up unweighting.

Stay on moderate terrain for the most part. If you go to more challenging slopes with friends, don't be embarrassed to stem when and if you need to. The stem is a good safety valve.

6J.1
DOWN AND READY

6J.7
GET READY FOR THE NEXT TURN

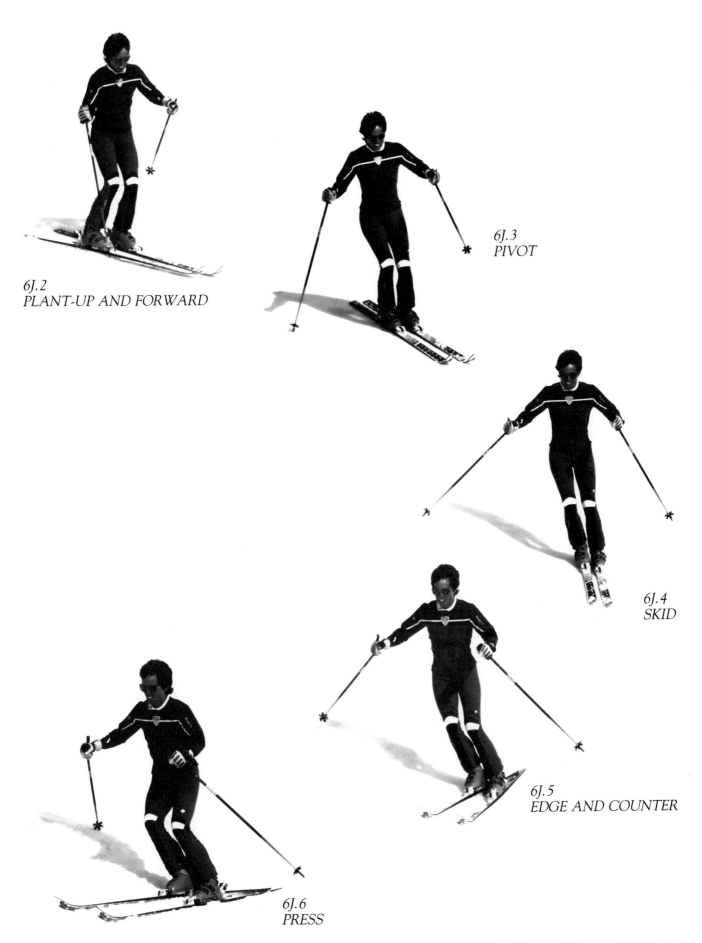

6J.2
PLANT-UP AND FORWARD

6J.3
PIVOT

6J.4
SKID

6J.5
EDGE AND COUNTER

6J.6
PRESS

6K.1
DOWN TO PLANT

Linked Parallel Turns

As you gain confidence you should try to connect parallel turns. At this point your skiing pattern goes something like this: down . . .up . . . down . . . prepare . . . down . . . up . . . down . . . prepare. Hear the hesitation?

If you can make the down motion that ends your first turn become the up unweighting movement for the next, you can modify your rhythm to be more like this: down . . . up . . . down . . . up . . . down.

This is really nothing new. If you are leading with your uphill side, you should always be looking downhill toward your new turn. Sink and get ready to plant all at once. [6K.1]

As you come up, move forward and toward the fall line with your upper body. This will help you start the turn. Your body is moving out from over your feet at the same time your feet are moving out from under your body. This will help you get to an edge quickly. Transfer weight now. [6K.2]

Turn, edge and press in the same motion. Follow through with your outside arm so the pole tip is already starting to move forward for the next turn. Stay countered so you're facing the upcoming turn. [6K.3]

Transfer your weight early if you like—before you rise up and into the new turn. [6K.4]

As you come back down in a turning and edging mode, weight will be on the outside ski, and your inside ski will be very light.

6K.4
UP

6K.5
TURN . . .

6K.2
UP AND INTO THE TURN

6K.3
DOWN

If you turn both legs at the same time, your inside ski might turn somewhat faster than your outside ski, which has more pressure on it. Your skis, in other words, might not stay totally parallel. This is perfectly normal. [6K.5]

Round off the bottom of the turn. As always, pressure is greatest at the end of a turn. There will also be deceleration here as the skis come out of the fall line. The friction at your edges, and the slowing of the skis will pull you lower.

Follow through with your outside hand, but stay countered. This down motion ending one turn leads into the up movement for the next turn. [6K.6]

As you may have noticed, this chapter covers a lot of ground. Some ski resorts divide "E" into several levels. E1 is called *Beginning Parallel,* E2 is *Intermediate Parallel,* and E3 *Advanced Parallel.*

Though some students cruise right through a parallel class, it's also not uncommon to repeat one or more levels of E. Progress at this stage of skiing is generally much slower than at the A, B and C levels. Moving on to higher E Class or to F should not be regarded as "passing."

More importantly, repeating a lesson should never be thought of as "failing." All of us encounter learning plateaus as we learn to ski, and many of us hit one here. Private instruction is often a very good idea at this stage, especially if you're having trouble.

Only when you start to link parallel turns together with rhythm and style, is it time to consider Class F.

6K.6
AND DOWN

Class E: Parallel Turns **105**

CLASS F

Short Radius Turns & Carving

As a parallel skier you may now think of yourself as a graduate student. You can also consider yourself an *advanced* skier, but keep in mind that *advanced* covers a broad spectrum. Students in F Classes, for example, range from solid parallel skiers to *very* strong parallel skiers.

It's for this reason that the F level at your ski school, like E, might have several subdivisions—F1, F2, and F3. As a graduate student you might join an F Class two or three times a season. Think of it as a "lab" or an advanced "seminar" on ski technique.

Whether you wind up in F1 or F3 on any given day shouldn't be a matter of great concern. One time the split instructor might put you in F2, and the next time in F1.

At the F level your instructor will also modify the teaching approach depending on weather, snow, and the capabilities of the people in class. What's more, at this stage different instructors place emphasis on different things.

As you move into the *expert* category, you will discover that progress is often slow and sometimes painful. There will be frustrating days when you actually seem to regress. But there will also be those times when you achieve startling breakthroughs.

You'll also discover that these breakthroughs are almost always based, not on some lightening bolt of insight, but on the building blocks of what you already know.

The cornerstones of your learning pyramid are the three basic skills of ATM: turning, edging, and pressure control. Only experience will teach you that, as you stack and arrange the blocks differently, you will get better at certain points.

For example, in Class A your instructor kept reminding you about your hands—to hold them up, forward and within your field of vision.

Your teacher wanted your forearms relaxed and your grip loose and comfortable. The use of your hands in class B, in C when you made your first pole-plants, and in D, were emphasized . You were reminded again in E. [7A]

You learned that if you held you hands properly, it was a simple matter to flick one wrist forward and plant your pole. In advanced skiing, as we've already said, your hands and arms become more and more prominent. Aside from your legs, your hands and poles are the only link between your torso and the snow.

Not only that, they are gauges that can tell you what your upper body is doing—for better or worse. You have learned that if you lose sight of one hand, something has gone awry in your upper body. (See Class D.)

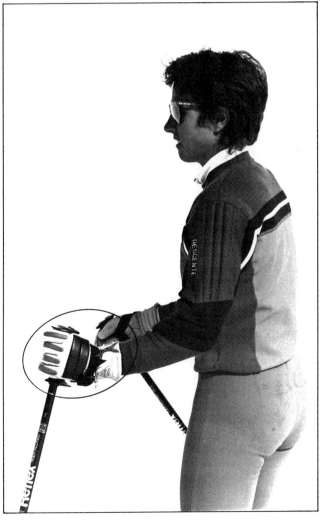

Your hands and arms must be free, yet disciplined. They should move up and down, back and forth, but always within a limited sphere somewhere in front, and to the side of your pelvis. Only rarely should your hands cross in front of you, passing over the skis.

The upper arm should hang naturally from the shoulder, and the elbow should not be cocked out as though you were carrying a watermelon under your arm. Most of the time the elbow stays fairly close to the rib cage. [7B]

You have already learned about *countermovement,* where the hips and upper body face down the hill, turned *counter* to the direction of travel. As you are countered, facing the way you arc about to go, the arms, quite naturally, remain part of the upper body. They must move with it.

Turning the upper body and hands above the skis and toward the next turn offers a number of options as to where you might plant your pole.

Class F: Short Radius Turns & Carving **107**

Draw an imaginary arc in the snow, from the tip of your downhill ski backward to a line at right angles from your heel. Your pole-plant will fall somewhere on this arc 95% of the time. [7C].

Generally, when you make longer turns at higher speeds, your pole-plant will happen toward the front of the arc. As you make the shorter turns you are about to learn, and as the slopes you ski get steeper, the pole makes contact farther back along the arc.

7C
PLANT YOUR POLE IN THE ARC

COUNTERROTATION AND HOCKEY STOPS

We already know that counter-movement is a delaying action in the hip (and upper body in some cases), which keeps us from overrotating and overturning. When we discussed it, you were warned not to confuse it with *counterrotation*.

Counterrotation is a turning force. We twist our upper body one way, to make our skis turn the opposite way. Remember when you were a kid, sitting on a rotating piano stool? You rotated your shoulders to the left, but your feet swiveled to the right.

By turning the greater mass of the upper body against the relative lightness of our legs and feet, we can turn. The turning happens *while* the counterrotation occurs.

The *hockey stop,* which looks like a hockey player suddenly turning his skates sideways to brake, is a good example of counterrotation.

When you do a hockey stop you will experience counterrotation, but you may not *feel* it intensely. Don't worry about all of the mechanics, just be aware that they are part of your bag of skiing tricks.

Hockey Stop Without Pole-Plant
Counterrotation can help us make very short turns with our skis parallel. It can be used in

7D.1
STRAIGHT RUN

7D.2
COUNTERROTATE

7D.3
SIDESLIP

7D.4
STOP

combination with up unweighting.

Ski straight downhill in a low straight run. Have your hands where you can see them and your feet open. [7D.1]

Rise up to unweight. At the high point of the up motion, use your stomach muscles to hold your upper body straight, so it continues to face directly down the fall line. At this point you may feel your upper body jerk ever so slightly to the right. At the same time pivot your feet to the left. [7D.2]

Sideslip for a short distance in this countered position. Try to adjust your balance forward or aft on the skis so that neither the tips nor the tails slip downhill. In other words, keep your skis perpendicular to the fall line. [7D.3]

Set your edges by pushing your knees back into the hill, and come to a stop. You should still be countered—facing down the fall line—when you stop. [7D.4]

Aside from what it teaches us about counterrotation, the hockey stop is worth knowing for its own sake. It's the easiest and fastest way to come to a sudden halt. If someone skis in front of you unexpectedly, and you need to stop suddenly, throw your skis sideways like this and make a hockey stop.

7E.1
STRAIGHT RUN

7E.2
COUNTERROTATE

Hockey Stop With Pole-Plant

Let's put some more building blocks together. Use up unweighting, counterrotation, rebound (Class E) and a pole-plant.

Start in the low straight run just as you did before. The skis should be right under you and fairly flat. Counterrotation is much more difficult if your skis are edged. Let yourself have a little more speed this time. [7E.1]

Stand up and pivot your skis sideways by holding your upper body rigid. [7E.2]

Stay countered as you sideslip, and keep your skis perpendicular to the fall line. Get ready to plant your pole. Reach downhill with the pole tip. [7E.3]

Stop the sideslip with a sharp edge-set. As you roll your knees into the hill you will sink down. The pole should be planted—well downhill from your skis—just as you come to a stop. [7E.4]

Take a close look at 7E.4. If you set your edges very abruptly, your feet would stop and your upper body might topple over—toward the downhill side. Yet the pole-plant steadies you.

Notice too how the skis have been bent into reverse camber, almost like a bow. They are poised to spring back to their normal cambered shape. At the same time, the sudden stop has compressed the muscles in your legs. They too are ready to stretch back to their normal length.

This photo shows all the ingredients of rebound. Carol *could* use the springing action of the skis and the stretch reflex in the leg muscles to lift her up and into another turn.

In fact, try making linked hockey stops with pole-plants. Instead of coming to a complete stop each time, set your edges hard as you plant your pole, then bounce back to a higher stance. You will see that rebound is like a passive up unweighting.

At the high point of the up, pivot your skis back the other way, using counterrotation.

7E.3
SIDESLIP AND READY THE POLE

7E.4
EDGE-SET AND PLANT

Class F: Short Radius Turns & Carving **111**

DOWNSTEM

A *downstem* is exactly what the name suggests. It's just the opposite of an *up* stem. To downstem we push the tail of the downhill ski downhill from us.

The downstem is useful for a number of reasons. For one thing, it gives us a chance to brake on steeper terrain.

Second, it can provide an edged platform beneath us from which we can rebound.

Third, a downstem with one ski prior to a turn, can easily become a way of checking our speed with *both* skis. When we slow down by letting two skis skid, then set our edges and rebound off the double-ski platform, we do what's called a *preturn*. We'll be getting to preturns shortly.

7F.1
COUNTERED TRAVERSE

In a downstem, when you ski across the hill, your upper body may be slightly countered. Get ready to move your downhill hand and your downhill foot at the same time. Your upper body must follow closely behind. [7F.1]

Briefly release the edge of your downhill ski and let the tail slip downhill. Re-engage the edge when your feet are separated.

Plant your pole downhill from you as you make this edge-set. For the edge-set to be effective (and to get any sort of rebound) you must also move your upper body downhill—with the ski that's being downstemmed. It helps to reach *way* downhill with your arm, pulling your upper body with it. [7F.2]

7F.2
DOWNSTEM TO AN EDGE

7G.1
COUNTERED TRAVERSE

Downstem Christy

Using a downstem before a turn feels good. What you are experiencing is rebound unweighting.

Traverse normally, leading with your uphill ski, boot, knee, hip, hand and shoulder. Have your hands ready and waiting. Weight, as usual, will be on the downhill ski. [7G.1]

Release your edge and skid the downhill ski into a downstem. Let your body weight go with it. Re-edge the downstemmed ski sharply as you plant your pole. With your ski you have created a platform for a rebound and have steadied your upper body with your pole. Your downhill leg will flex at the edge-set. [7G.2]

Rebound off the downhill ski, match, and pivot both skis toward the fall line. [7G.3]

Finish the turn as you would any other that uses up unweighting. [7G.4].

Review photo 7G.2. Imagine the downhill displacement of the tail happening with both skis. That is one of the ultimate goals of downstemming. A rebound off a two-ski platform is better than a rebound off one. We work on the two-ski preturn next.

7G.2
DOWNSTEM AND PLANT

7G.3
REBOUND AND MATCH

7G.4
EDGE AND PRESS

Class F: Short Radius Turns & Carving **115**

Uphill Christy To Pole-Plant Stop

Make a hockey stop going across the hill instead of out of the fall line. The crisper you make it, the better.

This will be different from the early uphill christies in the fan progression that we did earlier. It is faster, has a harsher edge-set at the end, and a pole-plant.

Traverse at some speed. Counterrotation will help you begin pivoting the ski tips uphill. [7H.1]

As you turn, you should feel your upper body working in opposition to your lower body. You might have the sensation that you are thrusting both heels downhill. [7H.2]

With most of your weight on the downhill ski, set the edges of both skis. Put some "umph" into this pivoting and edge-set. Plant your pole as you jam to a stop. [7H.3]

Your body will want to spring up as you stop, and if it were not for the pole-plant, gravity and your own momentum would yank your shoulders across the skis toward the fall line. If you didn't plant your pole, you would tip over.

Later we can use rebound followed by this sensation of falling downhill, allowing our upper body to "pull" the skis into a new turn.

7H.3
STOP AND PLANT

7H.2
SKID BOTH TAILS
DOWNHILL

Linked Uphill Christies With Rebound

There's a way to feel two-ski rebound without making a total commitment to the fall line. Find a wide slope, and make a series of traversing uphill christies.

Try to make your edge-sets rhythmical. We're gradually working our way toward linked *short-radius turns,* and *shortswing*—linked short-radius turns with edge-sets. We use these for speed control.

Release your edges with up-motion as you traverse. [71.1]

Skid, steering the tips uphill, while thrusting the tails downhill. Sink and set your edges with a pole-plant. [71.2]

As the rebound pops you up, transfer weight and use the unweighting to help you turn your feet toward the fall line. [71.3]

Let your skis glide toward the fall line, but don't point the tips all the way downhill. Begin shifting your weight back to the original downhill ski. [71.4]

Skid again, in preparation for a second uphill christy. Steer the tips uphill. Thrust the tails downhill with the help of counterrotation. The skis should pivot directly under your feet. [71.5]

Flex the knees forward and into the hill to set your edges again. The pole-plant and the edge-set should happen together. Snap from the skis and the muscle stretch plus the pole-plant should cause you to rebound again. [71.6]

Continue this maneuver until you reach the far side of the slope. Then turn around and do the same exercise across the slope in the opposite direction.

Take a look at your tracks. You will have made two snake-like lines across the hill. You have made a series of preturns without actually making a complete turn. Notice that your tracks turning uphill are deeper in the snow than those you made when you turned downhill.

This should serve as a reminder that, as always, it's very easy turning to the fall line. Not only do you have rebound helping you, you have gravity pulling you there.

And it *always* takes more effort to turn out of the fall line—back up the hill.

We can float our way into turns, but we need power, edging and pressure to finish them off.

71.6
SET AND REBOUND

71.5
TURN UPHILL

71.1
SIDESLIP

71.2
CHRISTY UPHILL AND
PLANT

71.3
TURN DOWNHILL

71.4
GLIDE

ANTICIPATION

This is a test. How many differences can you see in these two pictures? [7J.1 and 7J.2]

The skier looks very much the same, but in the second he has planted his pole. The first is a picture of countermovement. The second illustrates *anticipation*. The only difference is in the use of the poles.

The concept of anticipation is vital to advanced skiers, and ski instructors love to talk about it. Anticipation is yet another way to help us turn. Sometimes it's used in combination with up unweighting or with rebound.

Anticipation is sometimes defined as *pre-rotation* for a turn. The upper body turns to face downhill so that all the muscles criss-crossing the torso are tightened.

It's a little like taking the end of a wooden Popsicle stick in either hand. You can twist the stick in opposite directions. But when you let go of one end, the Popsicle stick untwists and returns to its original flat shape.

If you end a previous turn—or make a preturn—with your skis on edge, your lower body is held by your edges. If, at the same time, you pre-rotate your upper body toward the fall line—*anticipating* another turn—your body has been twisted like the imaginary Popsicle stick.

7J.1

7J.2

Now, you must also stabilize your upper body. You do this the only way you can—with the pole that connects your shoulders and torso to the snow. The pole becomes your stabilizer, a grounding device. [7K.1]

To turn, release your lower body by flattening the skis. The body, like the Popsicle stick, wants to align itself. The muscles in your abdomen want to pull you straight again.

As you rise to release your lower body from the grip of the skis' edges, your body untwists and turns the skis toward the fall line. Move down the hill as you get taller. If you rise straight up, the skis will accelerate out from under you, making you sit back. [7K.2]

In larger turns like the one we'll see next, you may consciously anticipate before each turn, as you preturn.

But in short-radius turns you may not be conscious of any anticipation at all. Because your upper body is constantly facing downhill, you are *always* in anticipation.

With each pole-plant, you steady the upper body as your feet turn beneath you. You up unweight or rebound, and the body torques the skis toward the fall line.

7K.1
ANTICIPATE AND PLANT THE POLE

7K.2
RELEASE AND TURN

7L.2
ANTICIPATE AND PLANT

7L.3
RELEASE AND TURN

7L.4
KEEP FACING DOWNHILL

7L.5
ANTICIPATE AGAIN

7L.1
CHECK SPEED

Preturn Christies With Anticipation

One of realities of skiing is that the faster we move, the more intense the forces and power we have to deal with.

You limit yourself when you try only to *cope* with these forces by resisting them. It's better to use the energy to *drive* you into, and out of, the fall line. More specifically, anticipation works better as you go faster.

Of course, approaching any turn from a steeper angle permits more speed. Your preturn or a quick uphill christy can be quite sharp, and may involve quite a bit of edge. The idea is to reduce your speed and allow the countering to become anticipation. [7L.1]

Pre-rotate your upper body toward the fall line. Remember that the pole-plant is the ingredient that distinguishes anticipation from counterrotation and countermovement. Plant the pole while you are most edged and compressed by the deceleration. [7L.2]

Rebound and up unweighting are entirely compatible. It's perfectly all right to use one to enhance the other. In this case Jerry rebounds off his downhill edge, extends to release his edges, allows his body to realign from the pre-rotation, and then changes his edges all at once. [7L.3]

As you come back across the hill, edging and pressure on the skis are increased. Try to look and think ahead. Avoid letting your shoulders and hips turn with the skis. Stay countered to anticipate the next turn. The outside arm should already start forward for the new pole-plant. [7L.4]

Here's a classic shot of an anticipated skier. The lower body is turned to the left, the upper body to the right. The bottom end of the "Popsicle stick" is held by the edges, the top end by the pole-plant. [7L.5]

When the lower end is released, the body straights itself out.

SHORT-RADIUS PARALLEL TURNS

Everybody wants to "boogie." Many intermediate skiers associate short-radius turns with excellent skiing. They *are* fun to do, and they require timing, rhythm and balance. Yet at this point you should not find them very difficult. If you can make a good parallel turn, you *can* do short turns.

The fact of the matter is, fine long-radius turns are actually more difficult to perform than great short-radius turns. Because the movements in short turns happen rapidly, they are easier to control.

There are many ways to do linked short-radius turns. You may use up unweighting, down unweighting, terrain unweighting, or rebound. You can rotate, counterrotate or anticipate. By now you have plenty of tools at your disposal, and there are lots of ways to do it correctly. You will continue to develop your own style.

Often, simplest is best. Here are two plain-vanilla short turns, done with up unweighting.

Remember that to come up, we must first go down. "Down" is usually the result of edging. At this stage we normally plant the pole as we go down. The pole-plant then triggers "up." [7M.1]

Anticipation followed by up helps us into the turn. Anything and everything you have learned since your first wedge turn can now come into play. Turn your feet, transfer weight, change edges. You won't have to think about it much. It will all just happen. [7M.2]

We learned long ago that if we want to turn sharply, it helps to use the sidecut of the ski. Increase pressure on the edged ski to tighten the arc at the bottom of the turn. All of this makes you sink down. [7M.3]

Always try to keep your hands moving in short turns. If you get lazy with one hand it may drop behind you and fail to be ready for the upcoming pole-plant. Be reaching for the new pole-plant constantly. [7M.4]

You don't need to plan it specifically, but if you're doing things right, your feet will go out from under you and come close together during the mid-phase of the turn. The outside ski is weighted and edged, and centrifugal force pulls the inside ski to it. [7M.5]

At the end of each short-radius turn you will feel your skis passing back under you before going out to the other side. Like a dog on a leash, they wander away and then return. As they cross under your center of mass the edges must be changed. You will feel the most pressure just before the edge change. [7M.6]

7M.1
DOWN AND PLANT

7M.2
UP AND TURN

7M.3
DOWN AND EDGE

7M.6
PRESS AND CHANGE EDGES

7M.4
PLANT AND UP

7M.5
TURN AND EDGE

Short-Radius Parallel Turns With Edge-Sets

A quick word about pressure. *Pressure control* is one of skiing's "big three" skills. In general, as our skill level rises, our skiing speed increases.

Up to this point we have created pressure on the skis at the bottom of the turn by increased edging, which meant more friction. As we edge, we normally flex, or come down. We have used the command, "press" to describe this flexion that accompanies a pressure build-up.

As speed increases, pressure increases proportionally. At a certain point, pressures become too great. The problem then is not to add pressure, but to relieve it.

Ironically, as we get better, we begin to use down motion or "flexion" to release and absorb pressure, instead of edging harder to create it. Our legs then become pressure-release valves, which prevent the skis from becoming *overloaded.*

Take a look at this long sequence.

As we've said before, skiing is holding back and letting go. We create edging and then release it. We let pressure build, then relieve it.

If we edge a lot in short turns the holding-back and the letting-go happen in rapid succession. In this way we can control our speed, even in steep, narrow places.

When we first pick her up on camera, Carol is flexed. By edging hard and turning the skis across the fall line, she has allowed a big pressure build-up. See how the ski bends. She'll use this to her advantage. [7N.1]

The bent ski can rebound and pass beneath the body once it's released. This is a good time to transfer weight—as the edges are changed and while the turn is being initiated with the help of unweighting. [7N.2]

As the skis drift out to the side, they naturally seek an edge. Once there's edging, pressure begins to build immediately. The pole must be in contact with the snow at the point of release, so keep that outside hand coming forward. [7N.3]

See the anticipation in the upper body, stabilized by the pole. The downhill ski is about to be released. Carol has allowed her stance to open. This lets her transfer weight, and flatten her uphill ski ahead of time. [7N.4]

The skis can be edged early, as soon as they're released on their way out from under the center of mass. The uncoiling of the body helps steer them downhill. [7N.5]

Again, the point of maximum pressure is just before the skis pass back under the center of mass. In linked turns the hands must never stop moving, and the torso remains anticipated at all times. This is the edge-set. [7N.6]

Rebounding off the edge-set helps the skis to flatten. As in all of skiing, when the skis are directly beneath us they tend to be flat on the snow. Skis must always go past flatness on their way to the opposite edge. [7N.7]

The beat goes on. Up-down . . . up-down . . . up-down. Holding back, letting go, holding back . . . [7N.8]

7N.1
DOWN

7N.2
LET GO

7N.3
HOLD BACK

7N.4
ANTICIPATE

7N.5
LET GO

7N.6
SET TO HOLD BACK

7N.7
UP TO LET GO

7N.8
TURN

Class F: Short Radius Turns & Carving **127**

MILESTONE #9:
SHORTSWING

This is a series of very polished short-radius turns—normally straight down the fall line. The amount of edge-set depends on the steepness of the slope and the hardness of the snow.

In short-radius turns with a lot of edge-set, we get the feeling that the skis pass beneath us and then out to the side before passing under us again. Sometimes, though not necessarily always, we are more aggressive with the upper body as we shortswing.

Instead of passively allowing the upper body to face and move straight downhill, with the skis swinging beneath, we might actively move the upper body out from over the skis. The sensation is that the shoulders are moving downhill slightly ahead, "pulling" the skis behind them.

As the edges are released, the upper body can be projected into the fall line. In other words, as the legs extend, the torso begins to "fall" downhill across the skis. [70.1]

When you move ahead of the skis and transfer your weight early, the skis move out from under you early as well. This causes an early edge engagement. [70.2]

Pressure can be at its high point when the skis are the farthest from you. By bending your legs (going "down") some of this pressure can be absorbed before the next edge change. [70.3]

At the rebound keep moving your center of mass down the hill, just ahead of the skis. Feel as though you are crossing over the skis as they cross under you. [70.4]

Edge and create pressure early, then release pressure and let the skis glide back under you. [70.5]

Continue to cross over your skis. Realignment after anticipation and downhill movement of the center of mass work together to pull your skis to the fall line. [70.6]

Show fluid movement. Keep everything moving. The hands never stop. Keep reaching for the next turn. You are always either in the process of making yourself longer, or making yourself shorter. [70.7]

70.1
MOVE DOWN THE HILL

70.2
EDGE EARLY

70.3
ABSORB PRESSURE WITH
YOUR KNEES

70.4
CROSS OVER

70.5
PRESS AND RELEASE EARLY

70.6
CROSS OVER

70.7
MOVE!

ANGULATION

Angulation is nothing new. You have been using it since you made your first turn in Class A. We just have not put a label on it yet. Many skiers are confused about angulation, mainly because there are several different kinds, used in different types of turns.

We understand angulation best when we look at another skier head on—as though he or she were coming right at us. Angles begin to appear at various points in the body whenever the skier tips the skis on edge. We refer to "angulation" when we want to describe the way the body bends sideways.

Speed, snow texture, terrain, the shape of the turn, the radius of the turn and forces involved in the turn determine which kind of angulation works best. Often various types of angulation are used in combination.

Knee Angulation

When we need to be quick, we edge the skis with our knees, tilting the lower leg bone. Knee angulation is really an optical illusion. The knee *appears* to be bending sideways, which it cannot really do without serious injury.

What actually happens is this: While the knee flexes forward, the femur bone in the upper leg rotates in the hip socket, making it appear that the knee moves laterally.

Knee angulation is used in short turns, and at relatively slow speeds where there is little pressure on the skis—as well as little force being exerted on the skier. We can edge the skis without moving them out from under us very far.

Although it's the fastest, knee angulation is also the weakest way to angulate. With knee angulation there is usually little countermovement. [7P]

7P
USE KNEE ANGULATION FOR SHORT, QUICK TURNS

Hip Angulation

Centrifugal force increases as we go faster. In a long, high-speed turn we must resist centrifugal force and gravity for a relatively long time.

When those forces threaten to throw us out of the turn, we have to get into a stronger stance to brace against them. We edge, and the hip moves to the inside of the turn. The knee bones straighten, reducing angulation. We appear to be in a tug-of-war with centrifugal force and gravity.

Hip angulation takes longer to achieve than knee angulation because there is more of us to move—farther. We can be stronger still if we counter the hips, pointing the belly button more toward the valley.

When we are counter and show hip angulation, the weight of our upper body is balanced on the top of our downhill femur. You can feel it standing still. [7Q]

7Q
USE HIP ANGULATION IN LONGER, FASTER TURNS

Upper-Body Angulation

You will see pictures of skiers leaning way out over the downhill ski. The curve of the body makes the skier look roughly like a "comma." Hence this used to be called the *comma* position.

Those new to the sport have never heard the expression, and might regard upper-body angulation as old fashioned. But upper-body angulation is still around, still valid, and still useful, especially when it gets very steep.

Notice how the normally-horizontal stripe on Carol's sweater slopes downhill. Upper-body angulation like this often accompanies knee and/or hip angulation. But it's used not so much to resist centrifugal force and gravity as much as to help the skier maintain balance.

All turns have a certain amount of skid—obviously some more than others. If you rode a street-type motorcycle around a corner on an asphalt road, you could lean into the turn confident that the tires would not skid out.

If, on the other hand, you were cornering a dirt bike on a gravel road, you would look very different because there would be plenty of skid involved.

You might lean the bike over, but you would take your inside foot off the peg and put it into the dirt. You would keep your body upright—staying above the skid.

Whenever we're in a skid we need to move *with* it to stay balanced. Otherwise, the skis (or motorcycle) will slip out from under us. In skiing we move the upper body out over the skidding ski.

We skid more in very tight turns. We also skid a lot when it's very steep. In both instances upper-body angulation in the direction of the skid becomes more apparent. [7R]

7R
USE UPPER-BODY ANGULATION TO STAY BALANCED WHILE SKIDDING

Total-Body Angulation

Let's go back to the motorcycle analogy. When we corner on a good road we "bank," knowing that the wheels will hold. We can bank on skis as well. When we do, the angle is mainly between the skis and the snow. We show total-body angulation.

"Banking" in this way is sometimes regarded as "bad," yet skiers have been doing it successfully for years. It's a good way to turn lazily and rest during a long cruise.

Keep in mind, though, that total-body angulation can be risky. If your skis should slip out, you fall on your inside hip. Make sure that snow conditions are grippy enough if you plan to bank.

It's also difficult to regulate the arc of your turn once banking has been set up, since it's all but impossible from this position to increase or decrease pressure or turning force on the skis. Once the turn starts, you're not really guiding the skis, you're sort of aiming them.

With total body angulation the shoulders and hips stay very "square" to the skis for the most part. That is, there is little or no countermovement. Total body angulation is sometimes known as *banking*. [7S]

Flip back through the pages of this book and you will see various types of angulation illustrated time and time again. Can you clearly identify each? Or does one blend into the other?

7S
USE TOTAL-BODY ANGULATION WHEN YOU KNOW YOUR EDGES WILL HOLD

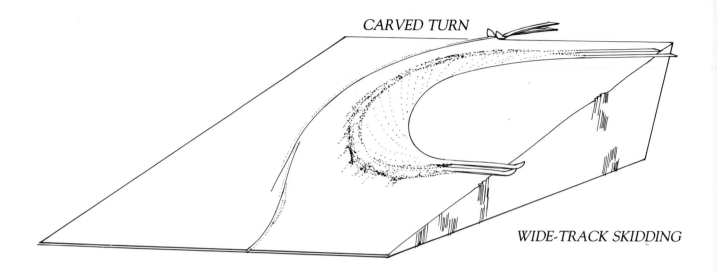

CARVED TURN

WIDE-TRACK SKIDDING

CARVING AND SKIDDING

"Skidded" turns and "carved" turns represent two theoretical extremes in skiing. A perfect, purely-carved turn is almost an impossibility. A purely-skidded turn is highly unlikely as well. If we did nothing but skid, we wouldn't change direction. All real turns fall somewhere between pure skidding and pure carving.

Neither is better nor worse than the other. When we skid through a turn, we leave a very wide track because the skis are turned across the direction of travel. The edges create drag and we slow down. Basically, skidding means slowing because skidded turns kill speed.

When we make a carved turn, we leave a very narrow track. The ski bends, allowing the edge to slice through the snow. To carve, the skier must flex the ski into reverse camber and take advantage of its sidecut.

As it carves, the ski points along the line of travel, and the whole length of the edge passes, for the most part, over the same spot in the snow. If there's any lateral movement at all, it's minimal. Basically, carving means turning without much slowing. Carved turns preserve speed.

Of course a ski can only bend so far and accept so much pressure. Beyond those two points it breaks loose and chatters awkwardly over the snow. This is why carved turns tend to be rather long. A ski can not bend enough to make a short-radius turn without skidding at least a little.

When we drive a car, the bottom of our right foot makes no value judgement about which is better, the accelerator or the brake pedal. Sometimes we need to slow down; sometimes we need to speed up.

Any car that can't brake is a menace on the highway. But so is a car that can't accelerate. Likewise with skiers. Sometimes we need to slow; sometimes we need to go.

For the sake of comparison, it might be worth taking a close look at both a simple skidded turn and a carved turn of about the same radius.

7T.1
FLATTEN AND TURN

7T.2
REGULATE THE SKID

7T.3
STOP THE SKID

Exploring Skidded Turns

Examine a skid from the snow up. The skis relate to the snow differently from the way they do in a carved turn. Angulation is different.

But all three skills still come into play. Turning may be of primary importance, but edging is definitely present. So is pressure control. The skier must *prevent* pressure from building.

Almost all the turns we have learned so far have been skidded turns, and what you see here, though exaggerated, will seem familiar.

To start a very skidded turn, the edges must be flattened and the skis turned. This might be done with up unweighting following a pole-plant. [7T.1]

Once the skis are pivoted into the fall line, some edging is required to keep the skid under control. *Too* much edge will create resistance and pressure. As they turn, the skis move laterally across the snow as well as downhill. They do not drift far out from under the body, however. [7T.2]

Because there's little pressure, and because the skis stay under us, knee angulation works fine. (If there's a lot of lateral drift during the skid, upper-body angulation may be needed too, although it's not shown here). Angulation creates edge, which stops the skid and makes the skis slide forward. [7T.3]

The sequence of primary skills in a skidded turn goes something like this: turn . . . edge . . . control pressure.

Class F: Short Radius Turns & Carving **135**

Exploring Carved Turns

The sequence of primary skills in a carved turn is somewhat different. It goes something like this: edging . . . pressure . . . turning. When we carve, we set up the right circumstances and the skis turn practically on their own.

To carve, we want to give the skis little opportunity to be flat and drift laterally. That means we must go from edge to edge very quickly.

An open stance to begin the turn helps. With his feet able to operate independently, Jerry can edge the downhill ski a lot, while holding the uphill ski pretty flat. He's ready to project his body downhill—across the skis. [7U.1]

Jerry extends, shortcutting his center of mass to the inside of the turn. The body goes out from over the skis and the skis go out from under the body. The result is a high edge very early in the turn. What we see is hip angulation. [7U.2]

With body weight settling against the slicing outside ski, and centrifugal force building, the ski bends under pressure. The pressure is controlled by the outside leg. Bend the leg to reduce pressure, extend it to increase pressure. [7U.3]

Because the skis are skidding so little, and very little speed has been lost, there are added G forces at the bottom of the turn. We are "extra heavy" at this point. Don't let the ski break loose, but absorb some of the pressure with your legs. [7U.4]

7V
USE HEEL PRESSURE

Much earlier, when we were still doing wedge turns, we discussed the way a ski is shaped. We learned about sidecut and reverse camber. Look at this close-up of a carved turn. [7V]

The "light" inside ski shows normal camber, while the outside ski shows reverse camber. This ski is bent about as much as it can be, suggesting that a carved turn can't be much tighter than this.

Obviously there is a great deal of pressure in a carved turn. The ski's tail, you'll recall from previous discussions, is somewhat stiffer than the tip. Also, the sidecut at the tail is not so radical. We will make longer turns if we put more pressure on the tail.

Carved turns *are* longer turns. To put more pressure on the tail, good skiers push through the heel of the foot rather than through the ball of foot while carving.

7U.1
PLANT

7U.2
EDGE EARLY

7U.3
BEND THE SKI

7U.4
HOLD THE EDGE

MILESTONE #10:
LONG CARVED TURNS

We've already suggested that long-radius turns are more difficult to perform well than short-radius turns. Because the turn lasts for more time, the movements of flexion and extension must be drawn out.

It's like operating in slow-motion. To make a smooth arc, you must show continuous movement throughout the turn. Timing is important. You can't, for example, run out of down movement before the turn is finished.

Let's look at a long-radius carved turn in more detail.

Because the turn is long, we don't need to whip the skis into the fall line quickly. As in most longer-radius turns without a preturn, there's little need for anticipation. Come into the turn low and fast. [7W.1]

To set up the carve we *will* need to change edges early, however. Extend and move the center of mass across the skis—downhill and to the inside of the turn. [7W.2]

As your center of mass passes over the skis, the edged skis swoop out to the side. Your hips are to the inside, ready to withstand the pressure that's coming. Show hip angulation. [7W.3]

As you feel pressure pushing against your outside foot, push *down*—with the rear half of your instep. [7W.4]

Let the tail do most of the carving. If you allow your hips to come square (uncountered) or press too far forward on the tip, the tail will break loose and the carving action will be lost. [7W.5]

Toward the end of a carved high-speed turn, gravity and centrifugal force team up in an effort to overload the ski. Use your outside leg like a shock absorber to suck up some of the pressure. [7W.6]

With experience, you will be able to feel when the ski is working well and when it's overloaded to the point of breaking loose. Regulate the pressure with your legs. Again, straighten the leg to add pressure. Bend it to reduce pressure.

7W.3
COUNTER WITH YOUR HIPS

7W.4
PUSH THROUGH YOUR HEEL

7W.1
FLEX

7W.2
CROSS OVER

7W.5
HANG ON TO THE EDGE

7W.6
ABSORB PRESSURE

Class F: Short Radius Turns & Carving **139**

SKATING
AND STEPPING

Two things distinguish the very accomplished skier from the merely advanced—*independent leg action* and an ability to hold an edge, even at high speed. In Class E we warned that skiing parallel was not the be-all and end-all of ski technique.

Skating on skis allows us to propel ourselves across a flat or downhill. It teaches us to thrust aggressively off one ski onto another. More important, it also prepares us for stepping and step turns.

We make stepping movements on skis in a number of ways and for various reasons. We can step from an edged ski to a flat ski. We can step from one edged ski to the inside edge of the other. Or we can step from an edged ski to the outside edge of the other. If you can step, you have all four edges to work with.

We step to increase our speed, to avoid something, or to adjust our *line*—the route we choose to take down the hill. We might also step from the edge of one ski directly to the edge of another to bypass the flatness that must occur when we change edges on a single ski.

Racers and expert bump-skiers step constantly. Sometimes they step into turns, sometimes they step out of turns. The more you learn about difficult terrain, race courses, moguls, and weird snow conditions, the more you'll grow to appreciate stepping.

Skating

When we skate, our skis are in a "diverging" relationship. They point off in different directions, in other words. It's very much like ice skating with extra-long blades.

The arms can swing, but the upper body should not turn back and forth too far. Face between your skis. [7X.1]

You will thrust off the edge of one ski by extending that leg, and glide onto the other. A ski is more or less flat as it glides. [7X.2]

As the glide starts to slow, flex that leg, edge, and extend *off* it. [7X.3]

As you skate faster, your tips must diverge less, and point ahead more. As you thrust off one ski you will move your center of mass over and along the ski that's about to glide. [7X.4]

Practice skating wherever the terrain permits. Skate to lifts. Skate across flat sections. Skate from lifts. Balance is critical. Try to feel a positive edge engagement and push off the middle of your ski.

7X.1
LOOK AHEAD

7X.2
THRUST AND GLIDE

7X.3
PUSH OFF

7X.4
MOVE WITH THE SKIS

Pointing (Converging) Step

A *pointing step* offers a high-speed, carved change of direction with a direct change of edges (step to the new edge). During the pointing phase, the skis are in a "converging" relationship and are on opposing edges. That is, for a split second you are on the inside edge of one ski, and the inside edge of the other.

As you approach a turn, think about being two-footed. You are going to step and point the uphill ski toward the fall line. Keep in mind, though, that you're traveling much faster than you are when you're making a pointing christy. [7Y.1]

Without losing the edge of the downhill ski, step the other ski out, and ready the pole. Extend the stepping leg as though reaching for the snow with it. Feel the edge engage. [7Y.2]

Plant your pole, and quickly transfer your weight to the edge of the pointed ski. The outside leg wants to be long at this point since you will brace against the outside ski. [7Y.3]

You can immediately start to carve. Press through the rear half of your foot. Your feet will come together. There's lots of centrifugal force now. Hip angulation will help you resist it. Hold your edge. [7Y.4]

The carving ski will bend through the bottom of the turn. Regulate the pressure on it with your outside leg. And if you like, get ready to step again. [7Y.5]

7Y.3
STEP OVER

7Y.4
CARVE

7Y.1
READY TO STEP

7Y.2
POINT

7Y.5
ABSORB PRESSURE

7Z.1
READY TO STEP

7Z.2
FLEX

Scissor (Diverging) Step

The *scissor step* feels more like skating. It lets us adjust our line to a point higher on the hill. It also allows us to accelerate into a turn by thrusting off our downhill ski. Racers scissor a lot.

Since the move is aggressive, the turn should be approached with speed and energy. [7Z.1]

Flex your downhill leg so you can spring off it. Make sure you have a good solid edge to work with. Start to guide the tip of your uphill ski further uphill. [7Z.2]

Extend off the downhill leg onto a gliding uphill ski. Face ahead, not toward the tip of the newly weighted ski. Your center of mass is about to move downhill. [7Z.3]

Let your upper body move toward the fall line—out from over the weighted ski. This will pull both skis downhill and bring the gliding ski to an edge. Begin to carve. [7Z.4]

Absorb pressure, if necessary, by flexing the outer leg. Hold the edge near the tail of the ski, and get ready to step again.

7Z.3
THRUST

7Z.4
CARVE

7Z.5
WORK THE TAIL

7AA.1
SKATE

7AA.2
FLEX

MILESTONE #11:
SCISSOR-STEP TURN
WITH POLE-PLANT

It takes a sophisticated skier to do a snappy scissor-step turn with a pole-plant—and do it right. It's the most difficult maneuver we discuss in this book. If you can do this well, you're almost ready to become a ski instructor yourself!

You will need speed. Come into it as though you were going to make a high-speed skating step. You don't want your skis to diverge too much. [7AA.1]

As you bring your pole forward, flex and get ready to push off the edge of your downhill ski. [7AA.2]

Plant your pole and thrust onto the uphill ski. Try to get some snap from your downhill ski. Remember that your body must move into the turn, it can not follow the stepped ski. [7AA.3]

Fall downhill to create an early edge change. [7AA.4]

Stay on the edged ski and let the pressure build. As it builds, push back through your heel to make the ski bend. [7AA.5]

Don't let the ski overload so its shape distorts beyond simple reverse camber. Reduce excess pressure by flexing the leg, but keep enough bend in the ski so it can unbend, rebounding you into the next turn. [7AA.6]

When you can do this, speak to us about a job. Happy trails to you.

7AA.6
REBOUND

7AA.3
THRUST

7AA.4
INCLINE

7AA.5
EDGE

Afterword

In this book we have just scratched the surface of ski technique. *The Way To Ski!* is by no means exhaustive, and was never meant to be so. It should be considered an excellent foundation only.

There are literally thousands of exercises used by instructors everywhere, which can lead you to the demonstrations you have seen on these pages. We're mentioned only some of them.

Furthermore, for the sake of continuity and simplicity we have emphasized certain techniques more than others. For example we have stressed up movement to release edges when down motion might have worked just as well.

As we said at the outset, we realize that there are many ways to ski, and at least as many ways to teach skiing as there are active, concerned ski instructors.

Knowing most of what appears on these pages will give you a large repertoire, as well as a very sound technical basis with which to pursue skiing. If you can make all of these moves well, you have become a very good skier indeed.

We would caution you about one thing, however. Although they represent an end for some, even the most advanced step turns only mark the point where skiing *really* begins. From this point on you are limited only by your imagination, but getting there will mean continued effort, concentration, and schooling.

Many of the finest ski schools have group instruction that extends way past Class F—to the G level and beyond. There are also many excellent certified pros who specialize in serving very experienced clients on a private-lesson basis.

Private instruction at the highest level can be the most fruitful ski lesson of all, and we recommend it without reservation.

Believe it or not, you are just beginning. There are an infinite number of skiing situations to seek and explore. You need to learn about steeps, about moguls, about powder and crud, about ice, about running gates, and even about freestyle skiing.

We haven't touched on any of these things yet. After all, they're the subject of another book.

Glossary

Angulation: Movement in a diagonal and lateral plane to affect balance, turning, edging, and pressure control while skiing. Described very simply as *comma position,* implying an extending movement in the feet, knees, hips and spine.

Anticipation: A movement in preparation for turning, during which the the upper and lower bodies are brought into a twisting relationship, stretching muscles and providing a quicker and stronger muscular contraction as the turn is initiated.

ATM: An abbreviation for the *American Teaching Method.* This concept was developed in the 1970s by the PSIA Educational Committee under the direction of Horst Abraham. It is distinguished by a reliance on the development of three basic skills: edging, turning, and pressure control. The humanistic quality of teaching approach is significant.

Backward lean: Inclining the body backward along the longitudinal axis of the skis. Also called *sitting back,* it's what most of us would like to do less of.

Banking: Deviation from the vertical body position to set up for, or compensate for, the effects of centrifugal force, and create the appropriate angle of edge engagement with the snow.

Braking wedge: A ski maneuver in which the skis are in a V position, and the angle of interaction between the ski's edges and the snow produces a slowing effect.

Camber: The upward bend of an unweighted ski that causes it to resemble a flat leaf spring. The cambered shape permits the ski to be weighted evenly along its entire running surface once downward pressure is applied.

Carving: A turning of the skis with little or no lateral slippage of the skis over the snow. Tails following in the line of the tips.

Centrifugal force: The force that impels an object moving in a circular path toward the outside of the arc. In skiing, it's the natural force that pushes our weight toward the outside of the turn.

Centripetal force: The force acting to hold a moving object in its curved arc. In skiing, the resistance between the skier's edges and the snow surface create friction to keep the turn going.

Checking: The active movement slowing or stopping the skidding of the skis by tightening the turn radius. This is a dynamic movement lasting for a short time.

Christy: A turn in which there is some degree of skidding and the skis are in a parallel configuration in some part of the turn. Example: stem christy.

Closed stance: Skiing with the skis (and feet) together.

Completion phase of the turn: If a turn is brought to a traverse or to a stop, the part of the turn effecting that change is the completion or finishing phase of the turn. It is generally thought to be the portion of the turn after the fall line.

Control phase of a turn: Middle portion of a turn where the skier guides the skis through the intended arc.

Converging step: A step in which the tips of the skis come together, as in a stem step.

Counterrotation: Turning the skis by actively twisting the torso and the legs in opposite directions.

Diverging step: A step in which the tips of the skis separate, as in a scissor step.

Down motion: Lowering the center of mass by flexing the joints at the ankle, knees, or hip.

Downstem: Stemming the downhill ski, usually accomplished by pressing the tail of the ski out until the edge bites and a platform is established from which a new turn can be started. This can also be used as a means of slowing or checking.

Edge control: Also called *edging,* it's the act of establishing an angle between the running surface of the skis and the snow. The purpose is to increase or decrease friction and together with the application of other basic principles, make it possible to change direction, accelerate, slow, or stop.

Edgelock: Forcing the ski onto a harsh edge by rotating the hip or leg. Causes the ski to run straight when the skier would prefer to turn or glide.

Fall line: The imaginary line following the greatest angle of the slope. The path a ball would take if released to roll down the hill.

Fan: An exercise progression where turns are made without a need to change edges, while working *toward* edge change. The eventual set of tracks is fan shaped.

Forward lean: Inclination of the body forward in relation to the longitudinal axis of the skis. Many skiers use this term when they are really thinking about projecting the body in the proposed direction of travel.

Gliding wedge: A gentle wedge position in which the tails are only pressed out a short distance, and the skis are slightly edged. There is little braking.

Hip rotation: Turning the hip, usually in the direction of the intended turn. May have either positive or negative effect.

Hockey stop: From the straight running position a quick pivoting of the skis across the fall line, and a stop by adjusting the edge angle to the snow. Similar to the stopping movement a skater would do.

Independent leg action: Using the legs in a sequential fashion to perform skiing functions. This does not necessarily imply a wide stance, but can happen even if the feet are close together.

Initiation phase of the turn: The portion of the turn where the edges are changed and the direction change is started.

Leverage: The intentional application of pressure fore or aft of the balance point of the skis. Leverage can also be applied laterally through the fulcrum that is the ski boot.

Matching: The movement toward aligning the direction of the skis after stemming or stepping to initiate a turn. Bringing diverging skis into a parallel relationship.

Natural athletic stance: Stance in which the joints are slightly flexed, the back is gently arched, and the head is up. Hands are usually away from the the sides, and the feet are at hip width or slightly wider. Also see "natural position."

Natural position: Standing in a way that supports optimum use of the body. Positioning is situational and will change with every change in terrain, snow condition and speed. In fact, for most of us it is not natural, but a learned stance.

Neutral stance: Standing so that the weight of the body is supported by the skeletal structure, without being forward or back, but in the center of the ski.

Open stance: Skiing with the skis (and feet) apart.

Parallel turning: The performance of all phases of the turn with the skis pointing in the same direction— parallel to one another. The application of this form is not limited to those who ski with their feet held tightly together.

Pelvic tilt: The angle that develops at the hips as a result of one side being higher than the other. Traversing causes one foot to be higher that the other and the pelvis to slope laterally.

Pivoting: Turning the skis about an axis perpendicular to the running surface. This movement is often called *swiveling* and is done on a flat ski. In pure form there is little edging involved and therefore little true change of direction.

Platform: Setting the skis edges at the end of a turn or a slip to provide a base for stepping, rebounding, or stopping.

Pointing: See *stemming*.

Pole-plant: Contact between the end (tip) of the pole and the snow. This includes a firm contact with the snow, or a touch, tap, or other form of contact that may take place at high speeds or in more difficult snow. The pole-plant is used for deflection, blocking, pushing, unweighting, balancing, and maintaining an awareness of the relationship between the skier and the slope.

Preparation phase: The portion of the turn in which position is established to make the next turn possible. This phase is often associated with the completion of the previous turn. Then one turn flows into the next.

Pressure control: The action of actively adjusting the pressure exerted by the skis against the snow. This includes such mechanics as weight transfer, leverage against the front, back or center of the skis, and changing the magnitude of pressure exerted through unweighting, absorbing, or pressuring the skis.

Rebounding: Spring back in response to the forces of compression exerted on the body mass of the skier, the skis, and the snow.

Reverse camber: The deformation of the skis in the longitudinal plane under pressure exerted by a skier standing in the middle of the skis. This is also called *decambering* the ski.

Rotary force: The force created by the torquing momentum of the torso and hips around the vertical axis of the body. Turning force is transmitted when the rotary movement of the torso and hips is slowed or stopped.

Rotation: The process of transmitting the rotary momentum of the torso and hips around the vertical body axis to the feet and skis.

Scissor stepping: A diverging step with the ski tips apart.

Sequential leg rotation: Using one ski as a support from which the other may turn. A one-two turning action.

Set: See *checking.*

Shortwing: Linked, short-radius turns with edge-sets. First described in German as *wedeln* or tail-wagging.

Shovel: The point, just behind the tip of the ski, where the ski is widest and where it begins to bend upward.

Side camber: The curve along a ski's sidewall that give it shape. Side camber, together with flex, makes turning possible.

Sidecut: See *side camber*

Sideslipping: Drifting sideways down the slope while the skis are pointing across the fall line.

Sidestepping: Walking sideways up or down the hill. The skis stay in a position directly across the fall line so they will not slide forward or backward down the ski slope.

Simultaneous leg rotation: Turning both legs at the same time.

Skating step: An extension from the inside edge of one ski followed by an extension of the same nature from the other ski resulting in a forward propulsion. The skis are diverging, but this movement differs from a scissor step through its emphasis on forward movement.

Skidding: A combination of forward movement on skis, together with sideways and pivoting movements.

Skills: In A.T.M., turning, edging, and pressure control, the skill areas in which all skiing movements can be categorized.

Sliding: Movement of the skis in the direction of their longitudinal axis.

Slipping: Movement of the skis sideways, at more or less right angles to the longitudinal axis.

Snowplow: An historic term for skiing with the skis in a converging relationship (tips together; tails apart) and tilted onto opposing edges to facilitate braking and turning. The action that results from being in a wedge.

Steering: The result of a skier's muscular effort to guide the skis along a desired path.

Stemming: (pointing) The displacement of one ski or both skis to a position convergent with the other. This results in the skis being on opposite edges.

Stepping: Movement from one ski to the other with the skis in either a di-verging, converging, or parallel relationship. Such steps can be performed from the downhill to the uphill ski. Involves stepping away from or into the fall line.

Step turning: During the initiation of the turn the skiers steps from one ski to the other and displaces the ski to either a diverging, converging, or parallel relationship.

Straight running: Sliding straight down the slope. May be in either an open or a closed stance.

Tail: The aft section of the ski.

Traversing: Sliding in a direction across the fall line.

Turning: Changing the direction of travel for both the skis and the body.

Unweighting: A movement resulting in a brief unloading of the skis.

Waist: The narrowest part of the ski, usually near the heel of the ski boot.

Wedge: Skiing in a position with the skis converging—tips together; tails apart. Wedge is the position, while a snowplow or snowplowing is the result.

Wedge change-up: Going from a wedge position, to a straight run, then back to a wedge.

Wedge turns: Making turns in a wedge position.

Weighting: Any movement that results in a loading of the skis. Push off in the beginning phase of up unweighting, for example, results in a loading of the skis.

Weight transfer: Shifting pressure from one ski to the other. See *pressure control.*

Bibliography & Suggested Reading

Abraham, Horst. *Skiing Right.* Colorado: Johnson Books, 1983

Abraham, Horst. *A.T.M. III Teaching Concepts.* Colorado: Professional Ski Instructors of America, 1980.

Abraham, Horst. *The American Teaching Method, Part II, Progression and Ski Mechanics.* Colorado: Professional Ski Instructors of America, 1977.

Alderson, John. *Captain Zembo's Ski Teaching Guide for Kids.* San Raphael, California, 1981.

Armstrong, John. *New Zealand Ski Instructors Manual.* Christchurch, New Zealand: J. and P. Litho, 1981.

Baer, Rudi. *Pianta Su.* New York, W.W. Norton, 1975.

Campbell, Stu. *Methodology.* Colorado: Professional Ski Instructors of America. Boulder, Colorado, 1977.

Campbell, Stu. *Ski With the Big Boys.* New York: Winchester Press, 1973.

Canadian Ski Instructors' Alliance. *CSIA Ski & Methodology Manual.* Montreal, Quebec, 1986.

Corwin, Larry. *You Can Be Good at Sports.* Chicago: Sports Training Institute, 1980.

Cratty, Bryant J. *Psychology in Contemporary Sport.* Englewood Cliffs, N.J.: Prentice-Hall, Inc., 1983.

Dougherty, Neil J., and Bonanno, Diane. *Contemporary Approaches to the Teaching of Physical Education.* New Brunswick, N.J.: Burgess Publishing Co., 1979.

Gallwey, Timothy, and Kriegel, Bob. *Inner Skiing.* New York: Random House, 1977.

Gamma, Karl. *Ski Suisse.* Switzerland: Habegger Verlag, 1983.

Gordon, Thomas, *T.E.T. Teacher Effectiveness Training.* New York: David McKay Company, Inc., 1974.

Hay, James G. *The Biomechanics of Sports Techniques.* Englewood Cliffs, N.J.: Prentice-Hall, Inc., 1973.

Holmes, R.J. "The Effectiveness of Visual Demonstrative Instruction versus Verbal Cognitive Instruction in the Learning of Snow Skiing." *International Journal of Sport Psychology.* Vol. 3, 1978.

Hoppichler, Franz. *Schwingen.* Colorado: Poudre Press, 1983.

Howe, John. *Skiing Mechanics.* Colorado: Poudre Press, 1983.

Jensen, Clayne R., Schulty, Gordon W., and Bangerter, Blauer L. *Applied Kinesiology and Biomechanics.* New York: McGraw-Hill, 1983.

Joubert, Georges. *How to Ski the New French Way.* New York: Dial Press, 1967.

Joubert, Georges. *Skiing, an Art . . . A Technique.* Colorado: Poudre Press, 1978.

Joubert, Georges. *Teach Yourself to Ski.* Colorado: Aspen Ski Masters, 1970.

Lawther, John D. *The Learning and Performance of Physical Skills.* New Jersey: Prentice-Hall, Inc., 1977.

Major, James, and Larsson, Olle. *World Cup Ski Technique.* Park City, Utah: Poudre Press, 1979.

McCluggage, Denise. *The Centered Skier.* New York: Bantam, 1982.

Mosston, Muska. *Teaching Physical Education.* Ohio: Charles E. Merrill Books, Inc. 1966.

Oxendine, Joseph B. *Psychology of Motor Learning.* New York: Appleton-Century-Crofts, 1968.

Radler, D. and Kephart, N.C. *Success Through Play.* New York: Harper and Row, 1960.

Sanders, R.J., M.D. *The Anatomy of Skiing.* Colorado: Golden Bell Press, 1976.

Shedden, John. *Skillful Skiing.* West Yorkshire, England: EP Publishing, 1982.

Singer, Robert N. *The Learning of Motor Skills.* New York: Macmillan, 1982.

Singer, Robert N. *Motor Learning and Human Performance.* New York: Macmillan, 1980.

Slusky, Thea D. "Warm Before Skiing Down." *SKI,* 45, November 1980.

Vagner, Juris. *Biomechanics.* Colorado: Professional Ski Instructors of America, 1975.

Valar, Paul. *The Official American Ski Technique,* Salt Lake City: Professional Ski Instructors of America, 1964.

Wagnon, John W. *Introduction of Modern Ski Teaching.* Colorado: Professional Ski Instructors of America, 1983.

Witherell, Warren. *How the Racers Ski.* New York: W.W. Norton, 1972.

ATM Sequence

To learn anything successfully takes time. Most of us need to review things we have learned to truly remember them. Here is a brief sequence to help you recall what we have worked on. We even throw in a few new items which you can ask your instructor about.

1. Remember the three basic skills of ATM
    A. Turning
    B. Edging
    C. Pressure control

2. Preparation includes the right clothing and proper equipment
    A. Dress in layers—stay warm and dry
    B. Sunscreen and sunglasses are important
    C. Boots must fit and be worn with the buckles on the little-toe side
    D. Know that your bindings work and how they work
    E. Go through the checklist of the things you need (lesson ticket, money, wax and scraper, etc.)

3. Get to know everyone in your class
    A. Warm up before you ski
    B. Remember your priorities:
        1. Safety first
        2. Fun second
        3. Learning last, but not least
    C. Terrain is vital to good learning—spend enough time on the easy slopes to get comfortable before you challenging the big mountain

4. Beginning
    A. Walking on the flat
        1. Start with one ski on; go forward, backwards, and in circles (For students with special needs you may do many of these exercises with one ski off. If this approach is used, give it enough time to be effective.)
        2. Do same maneuvers with both skis on
    B. Turning around
        1. Static exercises
        2. Pie turns
    C. Sidestepping
        1. Learning about the fall line
        2. How to edge
        3. How we step (any or all of the exercises may be done with one ski off)
        4. How to keep from tripping over your pole
    D. Falling comfortably and safely
    E. Standing up
    F. "Bull fighter" turn

G. Straight running
    1. Exercises
        a. Open stance
        b. Closed stance
        c. Weight on both feet
        d. Weight on one foot
        e. Alternate from one foot to the other
        f. High stance
        g. Low stance
        h. Weight back
        i. Weight forward
        j. Lifting one foot, then the other
        k. Moving one foot to the side, then the other
    1. Turning the feet
    2. Practice
H. The "gliding wedge"
    1. Exercises:
        a. Dryland wedges without skis
        b. Static wedge with skis on
        c. Hop to narrow wedge
        d. Press to narrow wedge
        e. Straight wedge on a short and shallow slope
    2. Practice
I. The "braking wedge" (If the slopes you are skiing on are very gentle you may want to make your first turns before learning a braking wedge.)
    1. Exercises:
        a. Hop to wide wedge
        b. Press to wide wedge
        c. Wedge change-ups
        d. Wedge to a stop
    2. Mileage
J. Riding a lift
    1. How to get on
    2. What to do once you're on
    3. How to get off
K. Gliding wedge turns
    1. Exercises:
        a. "Sneak" turn (think about making very small changes of direction—follow your instructor)
        b. Gently point (steer) your foot in the direction of the desired turn
        c. Follow the leader—long-radius gliding turns
    2. Mileage
L. Wedge turns on steeper slopes
    1. Exercises:
        a. Turning the foot
        b. Turning with the leg to create edge
        c. Driving with the knee to build pressure
        d. More wedge change-ups
        e. Transfering weight from one foot to the other
        f. Turn the ski
        g. Gently edge the ski
        h. Pressure the ski
    2. Mileage

5. Skiing across the hill—Traversing
  A. Slipping traverse
    1. Open stance
    2. Closed stance
  B. Traverse sideslips

      1. Reduce edge angles by standing tall (slip)

      2. Increase edge angles by moving knee and hip gently into hill (traverse)

  C. Holding traverse

      1. Practice standing more on the downhill ski

      2. Make a straight track across the hill by pressuring the big-toe side of your downhill foot

      3. "Perfect" holding traverses are not necessary

  D. Wedge turn to traverse

      1. Make a complete wedge turn then traverse the other way

      2. Link turns and traverses and increase speed

      3. Practice repeatedly to encourage a "spontaneous christy"

6. Wedge sideslips

  A. Cross slope in a wedge

      1. Emphasize weight on downhill ski to maintain wedge traverse

      2. Release edges with gentle up motion

      3. "Match" the skis

          a. Cross the slope repeating this exercise (wedge sideslip—match . . . wedge sideslip—match)

          b. Link wedge sideslip—match with a wedge turn and repeat

          c. Now try www e d g e match—www e d g e match

  B. Practice

7. Wedge christies

  A. Do ww e d g e match (a little faster)

  B. Do w e d g e match (faster still)

  C. Do wedge match (fast)

8. Intermediate christies

  A. Start to do more skid and less slip (gentle edging)

  B. Draw a quarter circle in the snow with your skis; make the skid rounder and narrower

  C. Start skidding sooner

      1. Up movement makes it easy to start the skis turning

      2. Down movement encourages edging and skidding to finish the turn

  D. Make lots of turns (Change the shape of the turns and match sooner.)

9. Pole-Plant

  A. Exercises:

      1. Straight run on shallow slope

          a. Swing right pole tip forward, flex at ankle, knee, hip and touch

      2. Repeat alternating hands (down—touch —up, down—touch—up)

  B. Practice

10. Intermediate christy with pole-plant

  A. Begin with a relaxed traverse

  B. Make a small wedge and turn toward the fall line

  C. Plant the inside pole (right pole for right turn, left pole for left turn)

  D. Rise and match, steer, skid and edge to a new traverse

11. Advanced wedge christies

  A. Pointing repetitions

      1. Stand tall in a traverse . . .

      2. Point the uphill ski toward the fall line

      3. Close skis, returning to a gentle traverse

      4. Repeat

  B. Drifting point repetitions

      1. Stand tall in a traverse

      2. Point uphill ski

      3. Weight both skis and drift toward fall line

      4. Turn back out of fall line, touch the pole, and . . .

      5. Match, edge, and start again

  C. Pointing christies with a pole-plant

      1. Stand tall in a gentle traverse

2. Point, weight both skis
3. Ready the pole as the skis drift to the fall line
4. Touch the pole, match, skid and feel pressure build on the downhill ski
5. Match earlier and earlier
6. Make the stem smaller and smaller

12. Parallel turns
   A. "Patience" turns—parallel turns without unweighting
      1. Start from a traverse with weight on the downhill ski
      2. Stand tall and weight both skis (edge will release as you stand tall)
      3. Ready the pole as the skis seek the fall line
      4. Touch, turn, and skid
      5. Edge and pressure the new downhill ski as you resume a new traverse
   B. Uphill parallel christies
      1. From a traverse . . .
      2. Rise to unweight and release edges
      3. Turn uphill and skid
      4. Edge and press forward gently
      5. Come to a stop
   C. Parallel christies in the fall line
      1. From a straight run . . .
      2. Ready the pole and flex in the ankle, knee, and hip (lowering body)
      3. Touch the pole and rise up
      4. Turn feet and legs
      5. Edge and press on the forebody of the downhill ski
   D. Parallel christies with a pole-plant
      1. From a steep traverse . . .
      2. Flex the ankle, knee and hip, and touch the pole
      3. Rise up
      4. Turn feet and legs as you transfer weight to the outside ski
      5. Edge and press forward on the downhill ski
   E. Practice
      1. Link turns
      2. Try to go from one turn to another with no traverse
      3. Enter the turn from a shallow and a steep traverse
      4. Try a little steeper hill

13. Shortswing
   A. Hockey stops
   B. Hockey stops with a pole-plant
   C. Uphill christies to a stop
   D. Uphill christies to a stop with a pole-plant
   E. Linked uphill christies with rebound
   F. Short-radius parallel turns
   G. Short-radius parallel turns with edge-sets
   H. Shortswing

14. Carving
   A. Explore long, skidded turns
      1. Refine turn and increase edge use
      2. Work on pressure changes (ski to ski)
   B. Exploring long, carved turns
      1. Edge the ski
      2. Pressure the edged ski
      3. Steer through the arc of the turn, using the qualities built into the ski

15. Stepping
   A. Skating—introductory steps
   B. Pointing steps (converging or "stem" steps)
   C. Parallel steps
   D. Scissor steps

Index

Health, Sports and Fitness Books
from The Body Press

Complete Guide to Prescription & Non-Prescription Drugs—Griffith	$12.95
Dr. Anderson's Life-Saving Diet—Anderson	$6.95
Fitness on the Road—Winsor	$7.95
Food Intolerance—Hunter, Jones, Workman	$6.95
Health Risks—Howard	$8.95 paper, $19.95 hardcover
High-Performance Racquetball—Hogan	8.95
Low-Stress Fitness—Brown	8.95
MuscleAerobics—Patano & Savage	8.95
My Body—My Decision!—Curtis, Curtis, Beard	8.95
PMS: A Positive Program to Gain Control—Bender, Kelleher	$7.95
Over the Hill But Not Out to Lunch! Over 40 and Still Cookin'—Kahn	8.95
Super Soccer—Hudson/Herbst	7.95
Stretch & Relax—Tobias & Stewart	12.95
Target Golf—Pace/Barkow	7.95
The Way to Ski: The Official Method—Campbell, Lundberg & PSIA	12.95

The Body Press books are available wherever fine books are sold, or order direct from the publisher. Send check or money order payable in U.S. funds to:

The Body Press, P.O. Box 5367, Dept. SKB-86, Tucson, AZ 85703

Include $1.95 postage and handling for first book; $1.00 for each additional book. Arizona residents add 7% sales tax. Please allow 4-6 weeks for delivery. Prices subject to change without notice.